TAKING
ADVICE

TAKING ADVICE

How Leaders Get Good Counsel

and Use It Wisely

Dan Ciampa

HARVARD BUSINESS SCHOOL PRESS
BOSTON, MASSACHUSETTS

978-1-59139-668-0 (ISBN 13)

Library of Congress Cataloging-in-Publication Data

Ciampa, Dan.
    Taking advice : how leaders get good council and use it wisely / Dan Ciampa.
        p. cm.
    ISBN 10 1-59139-668-9
    1. Leadership. 2. Management. 3. Organizational change. 4. Executive ability.
I. Title.
    HD57.7.C532 2006
    658.4'092--dc22

                                                            2006002372

*To O. B. Nelson, who throughout his life
overcame every hurdle put in his way
with determination, character, and a
level of humility most of us
can only hope for.*

Contents

Preface

THE TOPIC of how to take advice and use it effectively has not yet gotten the attention it deserves. I've been on the advice-giving side of the equation for a long time, and have offered help to many people who are very smart. But I've met very few "smart clients"—that is, people who know how to make the best of the help available. Most neither prepare for nor actively take responsibility for conversations with advisers. Rarely do they take steps to make sure that the people who influence them have the insight, ability, and knowledge to truly be of help. And even if the advice is on target, its recipients often end up without a clear idea of what they will do differently or how they will put to productive use what they have heard. The core premise of *Taking Advice* is that to be most effective, especially during times of change, the people in charge must be shrewder and more discerning advice takers.

Does it matter if a leader is adept at using help? It matters if the leader has to get it right the first time because there is little margin for error. It matters if there is insufficient experience or capability within the organization. And it matters particularly if the consequences are so important that a poor outcome could jeopardize the leader's career, the livelihoods of employees, and the trust of customers and investors who expect what has been promised. It is for leaders in these situations that I offer this book. The chapters that follow will examine advice taking as a skill and offer a way to think about this complicated and necessary task.

Insights from the Supply Side

My first exposure to the supply side of advice was as an undergraduate in the late 1960s, when I co-founded a leadership-training program that several other universities and a few community social-service agencies asked for help replicating. At nineteen years old, I had my first taste of advice giving. After graduation I was hired by a pioneering organizational-research and management-training firm, where I learned from people who had helped create the discipline of organization development and what had become the standard approaches to developing management talent and understanding organization culture.[1] This firm, the Behavioral Science Center of Sterling Institute (which soon became McBer & Co.) represented an early attempt to make research on motivation, group behavior, and organization design actionable through projects for the U.S. government, non-government entities, and not-for-profit organizations. I worked in economic development, community action, conflict resolution and teamwork, management development, and organization assessment. I also worked with venture-capital companies assessing the management of startups that they were considering for investment. I was trained in the leading management and organization-development programs of the time. All of this set the stage for the second phase of my career, beginning in 1972: operations problem solving and process improvement.

When I entered management consulting in the early 1970s, it was still a small profession. Young people in entry-level jobs could expect a guild-like apprenticeship, complete with examinations and peer reviews, to progress from one level to the next. Consultants asked themselves whether they had genuinely earned their fees, and wouldn't bill the client if the honest answer was no. After completion of a project, teams would return to the client periodically at no charge to assess the efficacy of their work (and not in an effort to sell another project). It sounds quaint, but it worked for a long time.

The firm I joined in 1972, Rath & Strong, was among the best at solving complicated product-design, production, efficiency, and distribution problems for large manufacturing companies. Since its founding in 1935, it had established a position in American manufacturing that combined the specialized technical expertise of Arthur D. Little with the broader management-process discipline of James McKinsey, two founders of the consulting profession as we know it today. Rath and Strong's philosophy of advice giving was founded on the core principles that (1) consultants should offer specific expertise and deep experience, (2) consulting should be a fulfilling career worthy of a long-term commitment, and (3) as in any helping profession, the emphasis should be on providing clients the means to solve their most important problems. Billing, firm growth, and competition with other firms were subordinate considerations.

I had been hired to help bring about what would be the first merger of technical and process improvement with organization development. One side possessed proven ways to assure product quality and reliability, efficiency and cost control, production flow, inventory management, and product design; the other side knew how to involve employees, improve cross-unit collaboration, adapt organizational structures, and train managers to instill a habit of continuous improvement. Combining the two types of expertise could generate better and longer-lasting solutions to tough operations problems than either approach could achieve alone. It could also point the way toward more innovative, continually improving organizations. We were the first consulting firm to succeed at this cross-disciplinary approach. Over the next twelve years, I directed dozens of large multiyear projects to change the technologies, manufacturing processes, and cultures of companies in many industries. As in the first phase of my career, I was fortunate again to be challenged and taught by creators and leading thinkers in the fields I worked in: quality and reliability engineering, product development, inventory management, labor relations, efficiency and cost containment, and process improvement.[2]

This was an era of great upheaval for American business. The penalties for not changing were extreme, and the reward for getting it right was to remain competitive. The Total Quality approach to running an enterprise, along with the collection of techniques known as Just-In-Time Manufacturing (the precursors of today's versions of Six Sigma and Lean Manufacturing), had just begun to be widely embraced. Together they represented a significant departure from the way American companies had operated for fifty years. Deriving the greatest benefit from them required combining the best tools and techniques from the people/culture and technical/process-improvement spheres. Rath and Strong's cross-disciplinary approach had made it a leader in these new approaches. In the course of directing projects and advising leaders whose organizations were implementing these new approaches, I saw firsthand different styles of leadership and advice taking during times of fundamental change.

Experience on the front lines taught me something important: in the final analysis, what mattered most was not whether our solutions were grounded in the best research or our consultants were the most impressive experts. What mattered was whether the leader—the primary client— knew how to extract what was needed from the resources and tools that advisers made available. If he couldn't do so, the chances were slim that his organization could change how it operated thoroughly enough to compete in new ways. For manufacturing companies in that era, not embracing change could mean going out of business.

And so, in the early 1980s, having been on the advice-giving side of the equation for more than fifteen years, I began to search for a core body of knowledge about how top-level people listen to and take counsel. But I couldn't find a unified theory of advice. What I found instead was a hodgepodge of approaches to advice giving, lack of agreement on the capabilities that separated great advisers from average ones, and very different levels of commitment to clients. I began to record observations about the nature of taking advice and counsel.

From a Profession to a Business

Meanwhile, consulting was undergoing a transformation from a profession to a business as the supply side of the help equation became more concerned with its own growth and costs than with clients' needs. This change took place between the mid-1970s and the mid-1980s as the renaissance of American manufacturing generated profitable opportunities in a sector where the barriers to entry were low. Beginning in the late 1970s, the advice-giving business became both more crowded and more profitable.

The population spike began with the entry into consulting of large public accounting firms (then the Big 8). Facing the prospect of stagnant margins in their auditing practices, they recognized the profitability and growth potential of management consulting, especially if auditors could sell it easily by recommending the services of their management-consulting colleagues to their clients (creating conflict-of-interest problems like those eventually seen at Enron and elsewhere). Most of these firms built large consulting practices from scratch, rather than converting their auditors—many of whom had honed advice-giving skills—into management consultants. They were soon joined by software companies that had recognized the potential of consulting to help clients deal with the difficulties of installing the software systems they were selling. They offered high salaries to people new to advice giving. Some were right out of MBA programs; others were laid-off managers or technical experts. Some were management educators accustomed to delivering structured training programs but attracted by the idea of counseling managers struggling through the change process. Others were IT project managers looking for broader challenges as organizations upgraded their information systems.

By the late 1980s, consulting was attracting a large population with varied backgrounds but little experience in the art of advice giving. There was no agreed-on certification process, and training programs were rare.[3] This influx of high-potential but inexperienced people changed the way that help was conceived and delivered. Until that time, consulting projects had typically begun with a data-gathering phase conducted by the most experienced consultants, comparable to a physician's examination of a patient complaining of pain but baffled about the cause. Each situation was viewed as unique; the process of discovery was predictable, but each problem elicited its own tailored response. These consultants took pride in having seen enough similar situations to forge an appropriate solution, but never doing the same thing twice.

The influx of consultants without deep advice-giving experience, however, called for a new approach. The way had been paved years before by Bruce Henderson, who had founded the Boston Consulting Group in 1963 and created a new approach to strategic consulting. Henderson's business model had two foundations. The first was the invention of a template that made strategy more science and less alchemy, enabling the client to grasp potential strategic paths more clearly. Henderson devised a general theory of competition anchored by his elegantly simple Growth/Share matrix, which designated products as stars, cash cows, question marks, or dogs.[4] His approach revolutionized how a company was analyzed, offering leaders enormous potential value and fuel for innovation.

It also provided analytical tools to guide the inexperienced MBA graduates Henderson hired, which made possible the second foundation of his business model. In addition to a new way of thinking about competitive strategy, Henderson cared about the advice-giving capabilities of the people in his company who would sell and apply it. He had experienced a range of advisers as a client when he directed corporate purchasing at Westinghouse, and was trained as a consultant in the client-centered approach at Arthur D. Little. At BCG, Henderson hired the brightest and most analytical MBA graduates; he realized, though, that not all of them would become good advisers, and encouraged those who could not to join companies they had gotten to know as clients. The resulting career-path option was a recruiting tool, and people who transitioned through BCG became future clients through its alumni network. Henderson's goal was to end up with people who were both skilled advisers and smart strategists. As the consulting market expanded, however, most of the accounting and software companies with consulting units ignored this second foundation. They concentrated on developing "consulting products" and teaching their people to sell them, rather than training them to assess each situation, listen carefully for the client's underlying needs, judge the capacity of the organization to change, and tailor the best approach.

By the mid-1990s, consulting fees had increased dramatically—not just individual billing rates but the total cost of a project—as software, project management, and elaborate analytical protocols were bundled with advisory services. In pursuit of multiple ambitious objectives that had never been combined into a single project, companies were persuaded to spend unprecedented amounts of money on hoped-for solutions that had never before been attempted on a comparable scale. It was a gamble that did not always pay off.

Looking at Advice from the Demand Side

In 1984, after a dozen years at Rath & Strong, I was named chairman and CEO. Though we were leaders in an exciting field, parts of the firm were faring poorly. The changes we were experiencing as we adjusted to new client needs caused conflict and lack of teamwork. Not only did we have to stay on top of a growing market that we had helped create and that was now attracting much tougher competition; we also had to improve our own culture. We were getting paid to help clients solve problems that we ourselves were struggling with. I knew I needed help, and set out to find people who could advise me. I became a client.

I had already begun to piece together a comprehensive way of looking at advice, expecting that it would take a couple of years to write something useful. One reason it has taken so much longer—and perhaps why the topic has received such scant attention—is that help cannot be understood fully from the sole perspective of those who offer it. Up to that point, everything I had learned about the nature of advice had come from consultants and academics, people who did not have to live with the consequences of their advice. But our clients rarely reflected deeply on their advice-taking needs. If I was to avoid generalizations, I would have to understand much more about advice and counsel from the point of view of the person seeking help, and about his or her responsibilities as an advice taker. I began to record conversations with clients about how they approached their relation-ships with advisers, how they thought about their own role, and what they wished they had done differently when they had not benefited. I also kept a journal of my own experience as an advice taker during the dozen years that I spent as chairman and CEO. And I sought out people who had thought deeply about advice and counsel.

The period from the early 1980s to the mid-1990s, the years when I led my company, was a fast-paced time in the business world, especially from our vantage point. I'm glad I did it and glad I decided to leave when I did. I hired my successor, and after an eighteen-month transition handed the firm to him and left in 1996. I joined the boards of several not-for-profit and two for-profit organizations. Though I had worked extensively with boards, serving as an elected director offered a deeper and richer sense of the potential and difficulties of the board's special advisory role to the CEO. Then, just before September 11, 2001, I became a special adviser in the office of the Secretary of the Treasury, which offered a unique vantage point on advisory practices at the highest levels of the federal government during an uncertain time.

The time finally seems right to offer my opinions on the topic of taking advice. This book is not aimed at advisers who want to be more influential or effective with their clients. It is intended for their clients—

clients who should be more effective than they are at getting the right help from their advisers. It is for leaders of for-profit, not-for-profit, and public organizations who are grappling with tough strategic, operational, political, and/or emotionally charged problems. It is also intended for executives on the rise who expect eventually to find themselves facing the same kinds of challenges, and who want to begin preparing now to make the best possible use of the help they will need. *Taking Advice* offers an actionable approach to advice taking, designed to equip leaders to solve their most vexing problems through more sagacious, discerning use of advice.

The first chapter of *Taking Advice* sets the stage by looking at why leaders who are undertaking ambitious change initiatives almost invariably need advice, and how they can find the help they need and prepare themselves to make the most of it. Chapter 2 illustrates some commonplace advice-taking (and advice-neglecting) problems, as illustrated in five case studies of leaders in trouble. Chapter 3 outlines a theory of advice as a foundation for the chapters that follow. Chapter 4 describes different types of advice and chapter 5 presents different kinds of advisers. Chapter 6 explains the need for a balanced advice network and what can be expected from the advisers who constitute it. Chapter 7 delves into the attributes of the great advice taker and chapter 8 describes the keys to successfully translating advice into action. The book is filled with stories and examples, as well as more in-depth cases illustrating the full complexity of a range of leadership challenges.

Taking Advice examines four types of advice and four kinds of advisers, the attitudes and abilities that jointly constitute great advice taking, and success factors that together provide the key to unlocking the potential of available advice. A set of twenty-four case studies, distributed throughout the book, describes how leaders confronting a range of situations have managed their advice needs. With the exception of a few political leaders, including John Kennedy and Abraham Lincoln, these cases feature people I have worked with directly. Each situation is recounted more or less as it happened, though the protagonists' names have been changed. Some cases are brief, intended to make a single point; others are longer to describe a more complicated or nuanced advice-taking principle. Throughout all eight chapters, advice taking will be approached within a framework of overarching principles that will equip readers to think systematically and usefully about the challenge of taking advice.

Acknowledgments

When something takes as long to materialize as this book has, the list of people who should be recognized is long. First, of course, are the leaders I have had the privilege of advising over the last thirty or so years. They asked for, listened to, and in some cases suffered through, the counsel I offered. More than anything else, the relationships we formed as we struggled together to solve tough problems led to this book.

Some people who gave their time and ideas unselfishly also deserve special acknowledgment. Those who stand out in this regard helped think through the nature of advice and the responsibilities of the advice taker. At the top of the list are Bruce Henderson, Dick Beckhard, and Jim Richard. Alan Rush, a friend and adviser for years, has always been available when I needed someone to listen, and his research on advice shaped my ideas in the 1970s. Steve Rhinesmith's friendship dates back to our days together at Sterling Institute, and his critique of an early draft of this book got me on a better track. Chris Argyris supported the formulation of an advice framework over a number of years by reviewing drafts and talking on long walks through the old neighborhood. Jeff Miller always found time to be a sounding board, and Mike Watkins's encouragement for this project is very much appreciated. Malcolm Knowles's pioneering work on how adults learn and accept new ideas was very useful in the early stage of my efforts to understand advice. Arthur Turner was one of the first to point out the complexities of the advisory relationship in his course at the Harvard Business School and was a valuable sounding board. Special thanks too go to Sally Stirling, Sam James, Jacques Krasney, and George Stalk.

As I was learning the intricacies of manufacturing and process improvement, and we were finding a way to impart to leaders the tools and techniques needed to redefine the competitive landscape, a handful of wise people helped shape my ideas about how best to offer expert advice. Those who had particular impact were Joe Juran, Edwards Deming, Dorian Shainin, Bob Barlow, Bill Leitch, Arnold Putnam, and Henry Parker.

Carl Sloane, Marvin Bower, and Jim Kennedy also contributed in valuable ways.

Of course, coming up with a framework is quite different from explaining it in a clear and accessible way. In this regard I am particularly fortunate to have Ann Goodsell on my team. Her ability to take a complex idea and describe it clearly, in many fewer words than I ever could, has made this book readable. Jeff Kehoe's persistence kept this project on track, and the team at the Harvard Business School Press did their usual fine job. And, as always, Erin Murray's help was indispensable and always available.

TAKING
ADVICE

CHAPTER **1**

The Help Paradox

A CONSUMER PACKAGED-GOODS COMPANY known for its management abilities and shrewd decision making, and for exporting leadership talent, launched an ambitious reengineering project with the goal of establishing world-class information-technology systems and business processes. Instead, the project damaged customer relations, strained relationships between senior and lower-level management, caused talented people to leave in frustration, and reversed the steady progress the company had made in all these areas before it began. The project had cost hundreds of millions of dollars and was over budget but far from its objectives.

After deciding to terminate the project in midstream, the company's president told me:

We spent more money on this one project so far than we have ever spent on consulting projects that were completed. And I have to be honest: we got absolutely nothing worthwhile from it. I'm embarrassed to say this, but the consultants told me going in that there would be some broken glass, but that they'd get the job done and be a partner with us through it all. They convinced us that the progress we were making on our own was too slow— that if we really wanted to continue as market leaders, we had to tear down what we had and then build up what we needed. It couldn't be done in our [step-at-a-time, incremental] style. But the managers and employees would

1

see that the end result would be worth it, and the efficiencies and cost sav-
ings would pay for it. They had a good sales pitch, but not the implemen-
tation abilities to do what they promised in our environment. The only
thing they were right about was the broken glass.

How could managers so competent and sophisticated allow this to happen? They had compiled a steady record of success by taking careful, calculated risks. They were accustomed to big, complex projects and managed operational costs carefully. Why did they leap into something so important in such a haphazard way? Why was it only in retrospect that the consultants' premise of necessary deconstruction appeared so gratu-itous and unwise? Mid- and lower-level managers, who were much bet-ter versed in the problems than the president, had been skeptical about the consultants' approach and capabilities from the start. Why hadn't the president listened to the advice of his own people? Why hadn't they voiced their opinions more forcefully?

Also, the directors of the company included sitting CEOs of success-ful companies and respected academics. The audit committee had been aware of the project before it began and had conducted regular progress reviews. Why hadn't they recognized problems?

Mobilizing Change and Taking the Reins

By the mid-1990s cases like this had become commonplace, and each raised the same perplexing questions. Because the answers to these ques-tions had the potential to shed light on the nature and shortcomings of advice, I began conducting an informal survey to find out how top ex-ecutives made choices about the use of internal and outside help to deal with important problems, and how satisfied they were with the help they received. The more senior leaders I spoke with, the more apparent it be-came that they were often disappointed with the results of large consult-ing projects. And they were even more dissatisfied with the advice they were getting from outside consultants and from people who worked for them, bosses, boards, and staff units like HR and IT. The survey ended up spanning six years. Over that time, I spoke to more than 125 senior executives of a wide variety of organizations about their advice-taking needs. These leaders belonged, by and large, to two groups.

Change to Maintain Success

The first group had held leadership positions for some time, and their organizations were successful and confident. The corporate entities enjoyed revenues and profits at the top tier of their industries, and the not-for-profit organizations were known for innovative programs and successful fundraising. But these leaders had become convinced that their organizations had to change in certain fundamental ways in order to sustain success. They envisioned steps that their organizations had had no experience with, such as acquisitions and alliances, or substantial organizational change that required different structures, people, and ways of behaving, or a new work environment.

In most cases, the leaders recognized before their managers did that staying successful is more difficult than becoming successful, requiring even more diligence, hard work, and capacity to change. They also understood that recognizing the need for change is only the first step in doing what is needed. For many leaders, this scenario means learning to direct and motivate in new ways while sharing power they are accustomed to wielding alone, and convincing employees to embrace new ways of doing their jobs that initially require harder work as they learn new skills. For everyone, it means altering comfortable practices and habits. Many established leaders face difficult decisions like selling off divisions or letting go veteran managers who cannot deliver what a new era demands. These were challenges these leaders were not trained for, requiring skills they had not developed. Their advice requirements thus became markedly more complex as they entered new leadership territory.

Leaders in New Positions with a Change Mandate

The second group consisted of individuals who had recently moved into the most senior position in the company or a division from outside or through promotion from within. They were expected to pursue a change agenda, in many cases because they had been hired to replace leaders who had not met growth or performance expectations. Their organizations were not failing; none of these people were in dire turnaround situations. Most of the organizations were performing adequately, but their boards or CEOs had concluded that they had to improve in fundamental ways to avoid future trouble. Most had experienced a wake-up call of some sort that eventually led to management changes and the arrival of the new leader.

These organizations faced many of the same issues as those in the first group, but their new leaders had to contend with extra challenges. Each of them had to take hold of an existing organization and learn a new role. If hired from outside, they had to learn a new culture, form new coalitions, win credibility, and establish a shared vision without the support systems and advice networks they had left behind to take the senior job. For those who were first-time CEOs, a top agenda item was gaining the confidence of investors and analysts, or, in the case of nonprofits, large donors, while winning over the board of directors. Most inherited senior managers who did not fit the new leader's vision but were important to his early success because of their institutional knowledge or the loyalty of their constituencies. They had to figure out the steps to meet the challenges they had inherited, and often they had to do so under the weight of high expectations from bosses, employees, and, most decisively, themselves.

Inherent Challenges of Changing an Organization

The more I listened to leaders in each group, the more apparent the similarities in their situations became. Their specific circumstances were always unique, and their individual leadership styles and philosophies varied greatly, but both groups faced new situations for which their experience had not fully prepared them. In each case, the stakes were high. A new leader who failed would sustain career damage and set back the company in its attempts to improve. If an established leader failed to sustain success, the accomplishments he and others had worked hard to win would be threatened along with his legacy. Both sets of leaders faced the same two overarching leadership challenges.

Managing Tough Tradeoffs

Most of these individuals were, and are, highly competent leaders with proven track records in getting their organizations to perform at a high level. But they found themselves in unknown territory with aggressive, tough competitors on one side and more knowledgeable, demanding customers on the other. To satisfy both, quality could not be sacrificed for the sake of cost, speed had to coexist with careful analysis, and tough decisions had to be made while keeping employees loyal and whole-heartedly committed.

Progress had to be made on two fronts simultaneously. The leaders had to achieve short-term profit improvements by dramatically improving efficiency through new technology, systems, and practices and a streamlined structure. At the same time, they had to ensure that a critical mass of employees embraced their vision, followed their lead, and were motivated to learn new ways of working. People were being asked to do more with fewer resources and to meet increasingly tough targets. Without mastering these tradeoffs, the leaders worried, even the best their organizations could do would not be good enough.

Managing Oneself

The second challenge was managing themselves—their energies, temperaments, work processes, priorities, and relationships—to conserve time, fend off stress, and accomplish all that was necessary. Whether or not they had occupied leadership roles for a long time, these people were under immense stress. Change is stressful for everyone, but it is magnified for leaders. They routinely have to choose between imperfect options on the basis of limited information, and the decisions they made have significant implications but uncertain consequences. Their judgments have to be wise and discerning all the time. Unchecked stress is incompatible with wisdom and discernment, and—because their organizations have reached decisive crossroads—a few wrong decisions could have disastrous long-term effects.

Some of these leaders' personal work habits or experience were not geared to the pace of change or the decisions they faced. Some who were more comfortable dealing with one big strategic issue at a time instead faced many smaller operational problems. Some who were more analytical than inspirational, having moved up through a succession of technical or corporate jobs, were now called on to motivate workers on the front lines in a plant or sales office. For others, the main source of stress was inherited people who lacked the experience and temperament to contribute but whose knowledge and experience prevented the leader from replacing them. In still other cases, the administrative system was unsuited to the leader's style or the change agenda. These leaders struggled to cope with information that reached them at the wrong time or in a format inconsistent with the way they made decisions. They had to work harder as a result and became frustrated at the inefficiency of their situations.

Why Even Experienced Leaders Need Advice

Is help necessary when changing an organization? Yes, when change must occur in interdependent departments, business units, and organizational levels simultaneously. Help is also called for when uncertain choices with profound consequences require tradeoffs among speed, careful analysis, and the involvement of other people. Speed often sacrifices careful decision making and the full participation of the people affected by a decision. When facing pressured choices, it is imperative to proceed carefully and to involve the people who will follow up or implement—but it is at precisely those times that decisions must be made fast.

In complex situations, no leader—even one who has successfully led his company to new heights—has the objectivity to know what to do and how to do it all the time, and also to ensure that the managers who report to him do the same in their units. No one is knowledgeable, smart, tough, and experienced enough to consistently do what is necessary in these situations all alone. Even in an organization with a record of success, managers are likely to be satisfied with the capabilities and systems that have contributed to that success. Though they may grasp the need for fundamental change, they will continue to be drawn to the tried-and-true methods that have worked for them in the past.

In such cases, the leader must be alert to early warning signs of complacency or resistance. But his time is usually taken up with plotting the future and running the organization day to day. The leader must figure out and control the components of the change agenda, and often convince employees and others of their value, while also handling normal day-to-day managerial tasks and occasional crises. Because he has much to do in a limited time, help is often needed to assess how prepared his key people are for change. Experienced leaders' needs for help are different but just as urgent as those of new leaders.

Leaders in both situations must also expect to undergo some changes themselves. They will already have developed a leadership style burnished by past wins and honed by a few losses. But guiding an organization to become something new calls for adapting how they make decisions, approach strategic choices, and manage their senior teams to reflect increased complexity, larger scope, and other changes generated by success. They must convince senior people to shake up their own styles, as well as the systems and processes they control, and ensure that mid-level managers do the same with their people. And as all of this change cascades through the organization, the leader must make sure that what worked well in the past is preserved while new skills are mastered. In short, help is a must because the situation is unfamiliar and the challenges must be handled right the first time, and because success increases demands on the leader while shrinking the time available for mastering new skills.

A leader new to his job has much to learn and encounters innumerable barriers to learning it. If hired from outside the company, he can count on nothing to be as it appears at first. Before managers get to know him, accurate information about how things came to be as they are will not be easy to come by; many will tell him what they think he wants to hear, or what casts them and their views in the best light. Neglecting to find internal advisers who can offer a reliable perspective early on leaves the new leader in a vulnerable position.

Another hurdle may arise within the new leader himself. Consider a leader who arrives at a new company from a different industry. He enters an unknown environment without a support system and may have to relocate his family and attend to their heightened needs while assuming new managerial challenges. At work he will have to master a new set of products, new customer needs, and perhaps new technology. And there is the ever-present necessity of managing the expectations of new bosses, peers, and subordinates while projecting confidence that the hiring decision was the right one. The resulting stress can lead to less-than-optimal decisions at a time when it is important to make a good first impression.

The right help used in the right way mitigates stress. For some, the highest priority is help distinguishing what must be learned right away from what can wait. For others, it is sizing up the political environment: the leader needs another set of eyes and ears to pick up what she may not yet be able to. Sometimes the highest priority is simply someone trustworthy to talk to who can help clarify the options that lie ahead.

The Help Paradox

Most of the leaders I spoke with had in fact sought out help. Some talked informally with former bosses who had retired. Some approached professors they had known in business school. Others made overtures to senior-level partners at consulting or law firms they were using for other tasks. Advice also came from board members, colleagues, subordinates, spouses, and friends.

At first blush, it seemed that each group could be helpful. The retired executives knew the organization's capabilities and limits and had faced similar challenges themselves. Board members were familiar with both the organization and the leader. Headquarters staff people were in a position to see both the big-picture connections between organizational components and the details of how their function affected field or operating units. Spouses and friends were those to whom the leaders opened up and revealed their frustrations as well as their hopes. Attorneys and consultants, who were paid to help, could contribute analytical capability, objectivity, and knowledge of how others in similar situations had dealt with the same challenges.

Inadequacies on the Supply Side

But these leaders were largely unsatisfied with the help they received. Many said they had benefited, but all recounted dispiriting stories. Previous bosses acted as if they were still in charge. Academics offered simplistic theoretical answers to complicated questions. Colleagues turned out to be closet competitors. Board members lacked pertinent experience and were not close enough to the organization to assess the adaptability of the culture or what was needed operationally. Trusted friends offered sympathy but were too remote from the leader's situation to be effective sounding boards. Consultants and lawyers were married to a particular methodology, or made recommendations that were not quite practical enough, or had better marketing and selling skills than advice capabilities. Some depended on their experience and were not analytical enough to help in complex or intricate situations they hadn't seen before. Others had more educational credentials than experience, and relied on analytical models to the exclusion of human and political realities that defy rational analysis. Some did more telling than listening and came across as too prescriptive; others listened well but offered few actionable remedies.

When it came to the A-item challenges, these leaders received few tailored solutions that could be put into action and found few sounding boards who could facilitate their deliberations as they formulated solutions. The leader in this situation faces a conundrum. The stakes are enormous. The consequences of not getting it right the first time include failure of the change agenda and depletion of the organization's reserves, as well as damage to the culture and perhaps the leader's own credibility or career path. But she cannot do it all on her own, especially given the need to lead the organization's day-to-day operations. What to do?

My initial impressions seemed contradictory and implausible, but I gradually began to recognize and credit the existence of a help paradox. Though many sources of help were available to these senior executives—including more professionals, whose advice cost more than ever before—they were not getting the help they needed.

Shortcomings on the Demand Side

This help paradox will not be resolved until the professionals on the supply side of the equation do a better job. The conditions aren't yet in place for management consulting to be an effective and reliable source of great advice. There exists no industrywide consensus on standards for providing help, no proven model that distinguishes excellent from average advice giving, no certification process, no required training programs, and few organized mentoring efforts.

But as demoralizing as it was to hear how seriously the supply side had let these leaders down, I began asking myself whether that was the only reason that advice had not been helpful. Over time, it became increasingly clear that the answer is: not exactly. The advice business has glaring weaknesses, but what it provides will not change until its clients change. The right help is difficult to come by because of inadequacies on the demand side as well as on the supply side. In short, executives who want to receive better, more actionable help must become better advice takers.

What does it take to extract more value from the time, effort, and money spent on help? The people who ask for help must articulate better what they need and know how to judge whether they are receiving it. They should also become more aware of how their own attitudes and behavior impact their ability to take in and apply advice. In other words, they must become smarter about how they prepare for and learn from the help they solicit. That is the mission of the chapters that follow.

Three Fundamental Propositions

This book is founded on a handful of basic propositions. First, when confronting the challenge of changing an organization in fundamental ways, success depends on finding and making the best use of helpful advice both inside and outside of the organization. But not any advice will do. To be truly helpful, advice must be *actionable* (able to be translated into appropriate action), *timely* (because of the cost of not improving quickly), and *sustainable* (able to be carried forward without further extraordinary help).

Second, it is the responsibility of the leader to size up his or her own needs for help and to select advisers who are most likely to be able to provide it. Leaders dissatisfied with the help they receive usually have themselves to blame: they often find themselves stuck in advice-taking traps whose warning signs are apparent to them only in hindsight, though they may have been visible to others. Such traps cause misjudgments and faulty assumptions that can lure the organization down the wrong path.

Third, few leaders have developed the mind-set or the capabilities necessary to be great advice takers. They have not clarified and categorized their advice-taking requirements in preparation for seeking the types of advice that can be most helpful. Nor have they mastered the skills that will equip them to get the most out of the advice they find. As a result, finding and utilizing the right advice is too often a hit-or-miss game of chance.

What do these propositions add up to? That most leaders facing daunting challenges are unprepared to take advantage of the help they need. One reason is that they have no way to assess their advice-taking needs, and no frame of reference within which they can articulate and generate answers to the most pressing questions about finding and utilizing help. What are those questions? Among the most fundamental are these:

- What types of advice should I look for?

- What should I have figured out before I do so?

- How can I best understand my own advice needs?

- Am I aware of my own attitudes toward accepting help and how they affect my ability to use advice when I need it?

- What are the most common advice-taking traps? What warning signs predict them?

- What kinds of people offer the advice I need?

- What criteria can I use to select those who can help me most?

- If someone proves helpful with one kind of advice, how can I determine whether he can help when I need another kind of advice?

- When one person's help is not enough, what are the keys to managing a network of advisers?

- What do great advice takers do differently than others?

To become smarter clients, leaders need two fundamental tools: a framework for advice taking and an understanding of the attributes of great advice taking. This book will offer both. Chapter 2 will begin by exploring some of the commonplace traps that otherwise competent leaders stumble into when it comes to taking advice.

CHAPTER 2

How Good Leaders Fail
as Advice Takers

CALL IT the Lewis and Clark syndrome. It happens to every leader who decides that, if his organization is to survive, it needs to become something different than it has been. Sometimes it's because of a crisis that was dumped in his lap. Or, after joining the organization, he finds that things are worse than the recruiter or board let on. Or the organization has been on a roll, each year's results extending its successful run, and the leader who has guided it begins thinking about her legacy and decides to create something bigger and better.

In all these situations, the decision to change the organization lands leaders in unfamiliar territory. The cost of failure will be quite high for employees, for customers or clients, and for the leader whose reputation depends on the outcome. Going into the wilderness facing unknown weather, natives, and terrain, a wise explorer will reduce the risk of the unexpected by bringing along experts in navigation and communication techniques. On each leg of the journey, he will hire scouts and guides familiar with local customs who know from experience how best to proceed. But when running an organization, particularly a complex one, the right help at the right time is often missing from the leader's change strategy. Why? Perhaps it is difficult to anticipate what will be needed, since

FIGURE 2-1

Rules of advice taking

- Keep an open mind and pay close attention to the advice of people who may be more objective than you are. Make sure you grasp fully what they perceive and you may have overlooked.

- Never make an important decision on the basis of how it might affect your status in others' eyes. Doing so often leads to misreading or underestimating what it takes to succeed.

- Put together a balanced advice network. Avoid overrelying on the kinds of advice you feel most comfortable with at the expense of help mastering new abilities.

- When help is available, use it. Never allow pride or shame to get in the way.

- When a goal is so important that you are willing to risk a lot to achieve it, pay particular heed to the advice of the people whose support you need.

organizational change is unpredictable. Or perhaps the leader believes he can succeed on his own without help.

How does advice from insiders stack up against that of outside advisers? Both are necessary. Informed managers and employees in strategic spots can provide crucial advice on what will succeed and on the prevailing level of internal support for change. Outsiders' experience and knowledge are indispensable in areas that are new to the organization and when the leader needs objective feedback from an uninvolved observer.

What stops leaders from using advisers when they need help? How can a leader in a high-stakes situation access the right advice when it is needed? Are there commonplace mistakes that leaders can train themselves to sidestep? Are such mistakes avoidable? This chapter will address these questions by looking at five case studies that illustrate classic failures caused by poor management of advice. Though names and companies have been disguised, each situation is described as it happened. It is then analyzed for its advice-taking implications.

"This Was an Opportunity That Would Only Come Along Once"

Dave had been recruited doggedly for months by the board of a well-regarded company. At first he had thought that it was not the right opportunity; he told the executive search consultant that he had spent ten years working hard to win his position as COO and was on track to become CEO at his current company. The search consultant said that his clients, the lead director and the chairman, had spoken very highly of what Dave had accomplished and suggested a casual no-strings-attached lunch.

Two months later Dave resigned to become CEO of the new company, with a clear path to the chairmanship within eighteen months. "It came down to two things," he explained. "First was that I could be a CEO right away, but the big deal was that I'd be in line to get the chairman's title. Second, the chairman and the lead director really put in a lot of time with me. They sold me on this because they came across as really wanting me as CEO, and they made it clear that if everything went well, I'd become chairman. The chairman's job was mine to lose. This was an opportunity that would only come along once—I had to take it."

The chairman made three arguments that Dave found particularly persuasive: (1) The team he would take over was strong and experienced, with deep knowledge of the proprietary technology that key products depended on. (2) The company had been the most aggressive in the industry in expanding into foreign markets, and as a result enjoyed an advantage; competitors and analysts agreed that the mature domestic market alone would not generate enough growth to meet investor expectations. (3) The business was performing well, earnings were up, and there was no need for radical change. This meant that Dave would have time to settle in and learn the culture before grabbing hold of the factors that would translate into future growth.

Three Skeptics' Reservations

Dave had been convinced, but three people who knew him well had doubted that this was a good move. One was the CEO of the company where Dave had worked for ten years. The CEO had a vested interest in keeping Dave, but he was also skeptical about one of the board's arguments. "Dave said they had told him that being first into international markets was a winner, and that it was already increasing their top line," the CEO said. "There are two problems with that, and they're called costs and profit." He explained that Dave's new company's proprietary technology, while relatively new in the United States, was revolutionary in foreign markets. This meant building a service- and product-training infrastructure from scratch. "There was no way they were going to make any money offshore," the chairman went on. "They might get a lot of stuff going that would show up in their revenue, but it would take a long time for their offshore business to show a profit. Unless they had something up their sleeves that I didn't know about—and I told Dave that was possible—this so-called strength was something that could be a real headache."

Another skeptic was the head of human resources at Dave's old company. He had been helpful to Dave when he had encountered political problems and when poor relationship management had hindered his rise to the top. The HR head predicted that the culture of the new company would be problematic for Dave. "Everything I'd heard about it raised warning signs," he said. "We'd recruited some people from there, but they didn't last long with us because they were political in the way they approached relationships. Our guys just didn't trust them." He also questioned whether Dave would find useful help when he entered the new culture. "I know the HR person over there," he said, "and she's just not real strong on these sorts of things."

Dave's wife also had reservations. During the recruiting process, the chairman of the new company and his wife had taken Dave and his wife to dinner. Dave had enjoyed the evening and considered it a success. But his wife saw it differently. "On the way home, I was going on and on about what a great couple they were, and the discussion that the chairman and I had had," Dave later recounted. "But Sally said there was something that just didn't feel right—that the chairman had come across as a bit too slick. She wondered if what he said could really be believed and whether he could be trusted. I was surprised at that. But she couldn't really be too specific; it was a feeling that she had. I just let it drop."

Two of these three people offered Dave advice. His boss's advice was unsolicited: "He didn't ask me for advice and I didn't expect him to. But I thought it was important to let him know what I thought. The way I put it to Dave was that I worried about him making this decision if he was basing it on a false premise. But I didn't go into any detail about the international markets and how long it was going to be before they made a profit. I worried that it might come across as sour grapes. So I just said I thought it was the wrong decision for him, and that I wanted him to make this decision for the right reasons. I told him I was disappointed for our company, but that I was thinking about what was best for him too. He never followed up to ask me more about what I meant."

Dave asked the HR VP for advice when he was still weighing the pluses and minuses. "I told him that I wasn't going to try to tell him what to do, but that I'd try to offer a way to think about it," the HR director recalled. "His experience at our company said to me that navigating the politics of a place is not one of his strengths, and he needed to be careful. Part of his decision should be a careful look at the culture to make sure it was a place he could do well in. Then I went further and said that it might not be the best place for him, and he should at least slow down to take a hard look at the political part of it." Asked how Dave responded, the HR head recalled: "He came up with reasons that each of the things I said wasn't going to be a problem. He said the chairman had talked a lot about the values program he launched and that it was taking hold. And he'd met the HR head and they had hit it off."

A Rocky Initiation

Dave's first eighteen months were less smooth and uneventful than he had been led to expect. The chairman had been on target about the strong points of the senior management team, but he had neglected to tell Dave that at least two of its members had wanted Dave's job. Nor had Dave asked. The two disgruntled executives were strong performers who controlled important parts of the company, and tension had been evident from the start. Both questioned Dave's ideas, and on a couple of occasions they openly challenged him. It was clear that they had decided to behave as competitors rather than loyal team members. Within months, one of the two left to take over a smaller company and took several talented middle managers with him, including a rising star considered one of the best technical people in the industry.

Dave also found that the management team he had inherited was unable to collaborate to solve problems that crossed department lines. He tried to improve teamwork but made little progress. "This is a very stab-you-in-the-back kind of culture," he said. "I tried to get these people to be more trusting, but it's tough. I'm sure one of the reasons that stuff I wanted to implement took longer is because of lack of [candor] at the top. But I just couldn't get it to change very much."

Dave eventually accomplished most of what he had planned to do, but less quickly than he had hoped. What he thought he could implement within the first six to nine months took almost two years to complete. That would have been good enough to satisfy the chairman if the company's aggressive international expansion program had proven successful. But exchange rates and terrorism-related costs exacerbated the problems that Dave's old boss had pointed out—quality problems due to untrained foreign labor and unanticipated costs to educate customers and position products the market wasn't ready for. These problems postponed the profitable growth that had been hoped for. To make up for unrealized earnings that had been promised to investors, the chairman pressured Dave to cut costs aggressively and to release a new product in the domestic market before Dave believed it was ready.

During this period the chairman never acknowledged the promises he had made while recruiting Dave. More than anything else, it bothered Dave that he had been promised enough time to put in place what was needed for the long term and assured that the company's values were those Dave was used to. "I understand that stuff happens, and that things don't work out like you hope," he said. "But I put together my plan based on what he said. Making deep cuts would have mortgaged our future, and that thing about introducing the new product—I was really surprised by that." He added ruefully that pressure from his boss to ship a product before it had been fully tested would never have happened at his old company.

Dave has stayed at the company, with the same title and responsibilities, for almost three years. The chairman also remains in place; he says that he wants to stay long enough to make sure the international growth initiative is successful. Dave is still hopeful that he will add the chairman's title. His spirits sank briefly, though, when his former boss selected Dave's successor as chairman and CEO of his old company.

What Happened Here?

Dave made some decisions that may have cost him time on his way to the top. Also, his boss's decision to stay on may say more about reluctance to pass the company to Dave than about international growth. What could Dave have done differently? How well did he use the advice available to him?

Three people who knew Dave well and had various perspectives on his abilities all cautioned him that this opportunity might not be as it appeared to Dave. His boss (admittedly not an objective adviser) pointed out what he considered faulty logic. The head of HR cautioned that the company's culture and what it would take to succeed might be a mismatch with Dave's style and strengths. His wife was dubious that Dave's potential boss was straightforward and trustworthy. Each of these reactions highlighted a potential problem. Taken together, they seemed to warrant that Dave slow down and reconsider whether this was the right path for him.

Dave's boss and his wife offered unsolicited feedback; the HR head waited for Dave to ask his opinion. The boss and the HR VP also offered advice; both tried to be balanced in their comments and acknowledged a lack of objectivity. Dave explicitly requested advice only from the HR head. He did not follow up with his boss or his wife, nor did he act on the advice of the HR VP to look carefully at whether his style was compatible with the culture of the new company. In spite of the HR manager's warning about corporate politics, Dave seems to have done a poor job from the start of assessing potential political danger. He did not think to ask whether any of his prospective new colleagues, including those in positions important to his success, had wanted the job he was hired for.

What does all this say about Dave's ability as an advice taker? He made little productive use of the input he received. Even after a warning from the one adviser whose help he solicited, the political environment proved problematic for Dave, especially his relationships with the two strongest performers. The departure of one of them (probably because Dave was hired) hurt the company but improved things somewhat for Dave. It was easier for him to deal with only one internal political competitor, who gradually became less of an obstacle. But Dave's inability to improve teamwork is another sign that the political environment was tough for him to handle.

Dave's behavior was typical of people who are not good advice takers. He failed to follow up on advisers' allusions to problems that were more apparent to them than to him. He did not recognize that it was up to him to urge them to say more about what they perceived. Many people give advice in a hesitant way, especially if they don't have a long-standing relationship with the recipient or if they are concerned about how their input will be received. If an advice taker indicates by changing the subject, dismissing or ignoring an observation, or even through subtle body language that he doesn't really want input, most advisers will not persist.

Dave has not failed at his new company. He has achieved some tangible successes, and has passed the critical eighteen-month mark when most high-level failures happen.[1] But he didn't have to change jobs to make a contribution; he was doing so at his former company. The only reason he moved was to claim both titles, CEO and chairman—to direct both the company and the board. That goal was so important to him that he convinced himself he was closer to it than he really was. As a result, he was deaf to the people who tried to help him. And because of that deficit, he hasn't been as successful as he could have been.

Failure to fully take in the valid concerns of others is a common advice-taking mistake. Another is refusing help out of fear of appearing weak or incapable of taking charge, as happened with Rita.

"I Can Do This Myself"

Rita took over her family's manufacturing business when her father died. She had joined the company after graduating from business school; though her brother had worked there for years, her father had chosen Rita as his successor. "Brad and my father just couldn't get along," Rita explained. "It was clear when I got to the company that people were choosing sides. It was starting to damage the culture, and even caused problems with new-product introductions because people weren't cooperating. It got so bad that Brad took over sales and marketing so he'd be in the field and away from the plant."

Rita concentrated on the financial side of the company, contributing right away by importing new ways to pay down debt and manage suppliers. As she and her father began to spend more time together on the company, he shared his philosophy about the business.

My father was a distant man who kept to himself a lot. So when he started to open up to me about the company, I was surprised—and flattered a little bit too. He talked about the market and where he believed it was headed, about our competitors and where we had an edge or they did. Eventually he talked about how he had learned the business from my grandfather. My grandfather was an immigrant who came here with nothing. He started the business with another person, but lost it after a few years because his partner stole all their money. My grandfather had to pay off what the company owed and eventually started over again. But after what had happened, he never trusted anyone who wasn't part of the family. My father was taught not to tell outsiders anything about the company and not to trust them. One day we were talking about how to finance an addition to one of the plants and some new technology that required some pretty fundamental changes in manufacturing. I said that we should bring in some people who could give us advice, that someone who made sense on this topic had given a talk at business school. He gave me one of those looks, sort of a glare. He said that for as long as he'd run the company, he hadn't used consultants. If we needed something, he said, our people would figure it out—that he paid our people a lot of money, and they knew the industry and our business better than any consultant. It came down to trust and control. He was suspicious of people who sold their time, and worried that they would talk about us to our competitors or create a dependency so that we'd always need them.

Rita worked hard to learn the business, which became the centerpiece of her life. She divorced a couple of years after joining the company and had no children. On the professional side, prudent cost management and reinvestment in plant and equipment produced best-in-industry product quality and earnings and a stable and motivated workforce. Six years after Rita joined the company, it was more successful than ever but faced bigger challenges. Decisions had become more complex and she had less time to make them. The most experienced employees were retiring and being replaced by long-tenured subordinates who were not much younger. Meanwhile young employees left because there was no apparent career path.

Two years later, Rita's father died. His death was a significant personal blow; it was also a professional blow. Rita was in her late thirties, the top leader of a successful and growing company that was several hundred million dollars in size. But it had not invested in management development, and decision making and responsibility for strategy had been concentrated at the very top. Rita felt very much alone.

A Misdirected Search for Advice

Her father's will gave Rita control of the company. She briefly considered selling but ultimately decided to assume the CEO position. Her challenge, as she viewed it, was to maintain the company's growth and position in the industry while changing the way it operated to position it better for the future. Once she settled on that course, she decided she needed help. But she had no idea where or how to look for the help she needed. Her father hadn't built relationships with people who possessed the expertise she believed was required, nor had she worked with consultants or technical advisers. She also worried that bringing in outside help soon after taking over as CEO would undermine her image, particularly with the most powerful and long-tenured managers. Her senior managers were committed to the company, but she was certain that fear and respect for her father had motivated their past performance. She would have to earn their loyalty. But Rita knew that she would never develop the style they were accustomed to in a boss; she would have to define her own style. If she didn't do it well, she worried, she could lose control.

Influenced by her father's mistrust of outside advice, she turned to the company's lawyer. He recommended adding two local businessmen, family friends, to the company's board: a college classmate of her father's who ran a large real-estate development company and the company's long-time banker. The board had for years existed in name only, but the lawyer saw it as a vehicle for Rita to get help. She hesitated; though she was comfortable personally with both men, she was uncertain whether they had the experience to supplement her own. But in the final analysis, she concluded, it would be her actions, not the board's, that would sustain the company's growth curve. Rita also called a former business-school professor, who offered to bring in a team of graduate students to assess the company's strategy and capabilities.

Over the next twelve months, neither Rita nor the company performed as well as she had expected. Three events were responsible for Rita's disappointment.

A Series of Missteps

Rita lost an opportunity to acquire a small company with a promising new technology that fit her company's capabilities well. Though she had been the first to recognize its potential, the owner ultimately agreed to be acquired by another corporation. Rita was disappointed and angry at herself: her approach had provoked a bidding war, and the price had been forced up so high that Rita had had to back out. Nor had she involved her senior people, though they could have been helpful early on and could perhaps have brought about a quick deal. When asked why, she responded, "It was probably because I wanted to show them that I could do it, that I was able to make this happen, and show I could lead the company." She tried to do it on her own, and knew she hadn't handled it well.

In the middle of her first year as CEO, Rita became concerned about slipping manufacturing productivity. She asked the CFO and the head of manufacturing to analyze the underlying causes and make recommendations. Three indicators appeared to Rita to point to a root cause: equipment downtime had increased, the plant's housekeeping had deteriorated, and the shop floor was crowded with work-in-process inventory. Rita's father had prided himself on an orderly factory, and he would not have been happy with its current condition. Rita wasn't sure of the underlying cause, but suspected the top-down, command-and-control style of the head of manufacturing and lack of training and development for supervisors.

Rita was disappointed by the analysis she received. The head of manufacturing and the CFO blamed the productivity decline on late deliveries from two suppliers and high energy and raw-material costs. They characterized high work-in-process inventory as inevitable when a lot of volume goes through the plant. Rita doubted but did not challenge the assertion that more volume inevitably leads to more inventory. As for equipment downtime, she was told that a few machines had developed problems of a kind that "just happened sometimes" while others were being repaired; once repairs were complete, throughput would pick up. When she asked whether a preventive-maintenance program would prevent shutdowns, the manufacturing VP offered without enthusiasm to look into it. Similarly, when she asked about housekeeping, he seemed

unconvinced that it was important. Rita believed that the head of manufacturing was addressing her concerns less seriously than he should, but
said nothing.

As CFO, Rita had inaugurated a process for the strategy and annual
plan that required a high level of discipline. Her father had embraced it,
and the process had become a part of the company's yearly routine. The
current year's plan had to be particularly disciplined: competitors were
gaining market share, and Rita worried that neither she nor her top
people really understood why. But after the planning meetings, she remained unsatisfied. Rita considered the analysis inadequate, and only a
cursory effort had been made to talk to customers about competitors.
There was also a shortage of new ideas and creativity. What was needed
was new approaches to increasingly complex problems, but many of the
senior managers presented plans for more of the same.

Rita talked to the two new board members, but it became clear that
neither had the experience to help her figure out what to do. Meanwhile,
the team of graduate students presented their analysis just as the company's
planning meetings got under way. Rita hoped that her managers would
recognize the shortcomings of the plans they had brought to the strategy
process when they heard the reactions of objective observers. But the students dwelled on problems that were already obvious rather than underlying causes. They also emphasized problematic information sharing and
collaboration within and between departments without acknowledging
positive steps that had been taken. When the managers became defensive,
Rita realized that, as she put it, "the messenger was about to be shot because of the way the right message was being delivered."

Rita had kept a journal since taking over the company. Because she
had no one to use as a sounding board, she found it cathartic and instructive to reread her earlier entries. At the end of her first year as CEO,
she had written:

> *The big question is about me, not the company. It will do well—all the*
> *pieces are there because Dad put them all in place. My job is to make them*
> *work. Am I up to it? I heard [someone] say once that good leaders look at*
> *an everyday situation as a leadership case study—to look for the leader-*
> *ship implications in everything you see, like going to the symphony and*

noticing how [a great conductor] gets the orchestra to play together, to get even more than anyone thought out of the musicians. How can I do that?

The [failed] acquisition was a big-time disappointment, and it was my fault. I had it in my hands but I didn't make it happen. The big mistake I made was that I went at it alone. There will be other deals, and I'll learn from what happened. The big problems I've had this year happened because I didn't know enough or have enough experience to do what I needed to do. I am not my father—and even if I was, this current environment demands more than even he was able to do. But I didn't help myself either. I didn't reach out to [my senior managers]. They could have helped but I didn't bring them in. I was trying to show them I can run this company. Kind of sad, really, but there it is. I can't make this happen without them, but they don't respect me enough yet.

What Happened Here?

Why didn't Rita's first year turn out better? Rita was more self-aware and honest with herself than Dave was. Before becoming CEO, she had proven hardworking, smart, and creative enough to lead the company. Clearly, she was a prime reason for its growth and unprecedented success. She also correctly analyzed what the company needed to sustain success, and realized quickly that she couldn't do it all on her own. But she wasn't satisfied with her achievements or the company's results during her first year as CEO. Did it have to turn out this way?

Self-doubt shaped Rita's choices at critical junctures about the help she would depend on. She did not find the type and level of advice she needed, given her leadership strengths and weaknesses and the challenges that the company faced. Rita admitted that some of her senior managers could have been helpful in the acquisition, but worried that asking for help would come across as weakness and undermine her authority and stature in their eyes. It is unclear to me whether their involvement would have translated into a successful deal. If they could have made a difference, involving them would have been wise even at the risk of weakening her credibility. But Rita's failure to react when the manufacturing head reported about plant productivity probably had greater impact on their opinion of her as their boss. He was dismissive, even insubordinate, and should at least have been reprimanded.

Her second mistake was to select advisers who lacked experience and sophistication in the areas that mattered most. Neither new board member had faced business challenges comparable in magnitude and complexity to those Rita had taken on. They were loyal, and genuinely cared about her well-being, but their experience didn't equip them to be useful sounding boards or to provide expert counsel. It would have been preferable to appoint a third member to the board, perhaps a sitting CEO from a non-competitive but comparable company.

It was also a mistake to hand over a task that required experienced professionals to graduate students. There is nothing wrong with using a team of bright MBA students; their enthusiasm can be refreshing for an experienced organization, and they often ask questions that challenge fundamental assumptions and cause accepted practices and habits to be rethought. But the primary reason for using graduate students is to offer them an opportunity to learn, not to solve an important problem. Rita was right to order a review of the company's strategy and capabilities, but using people who had more to learn than to offer wasted an opportunity and was a poor use of the company's time. A better approach would have been to hire the best strategy consultants available and to pair with them the graduate-student team.

Another common advice-taking mistake is seeking help only in a sphere where one already feels confident, rather than where it is really needed. Consider the case of Barry.

"I'm More Comfortable with Strategy Than Politics"

When Barry joined a computer-equipment and software-development company as executive vice president and probable successor to the CEO, Chuck, he was in his mid-forties. Chuck thought that Barry had an ideal background to succeed him within two or three years when Chuck retired. After earning a PhD in mathematics, Barry had worked for a large consulting firm and then co-founded a startup based on an analytical model he had developed with a partner. The business was sold to a small company in Chuck's industry, where Barry became senior vice president of technology and business development. Impressed by Barry's technical background and entrepreneurial experience, Chuck recruited him away even though Barry had never worked in a company the size of Chuck's. Chuck believed that he could teach Barry whatever he did not know about managing a large, complex organization.

Under Chuck, the company had become one of the powerhouses of its industry. It had previously been a middle-of-the-pack player posting respectable, dependable, but not impressive earnings. When Chuck had been chairman and CEO for two years, things had picked up; over the next decade, the company had grown impressively. When Chuck and the board had agreed on his retirement date, the lead director and the head of the governance committee had asked him to draw up a succession plan and an exit strategy. Having concluded that there was no suitable successor within the company, Chuck told the board that he would initiate a search for someone to come in as a senior vice president. He would work with that person for two or three years, and then, if no current employee emerged as a contender and the board agreed, he would hand over the reins.

Competition and Organizational Hurdles

Several months after Barry joined the company, Chuck told him about the reorganization he had in mind. Though he had brought Barry into the decision-making process early, Barry could see that Chuck's mind was pretty well made up. The reorganization was implemented by Barry's one-year anniversary.

Six months later, Barry was doing well on some fronts but struggling on others. The company's managers believed themselves to be the best in their industry, and most were still unconvinced that Barry was indispensable to the company, particularly as the designated successor. Even if Barry had been universally acknowledged as the ideal person to lead the company, its top managers would have found ways to test him. Chuck was unsurprised by the behavior of the senior people, at least one of whom had expected the job that Barry had been hired to fill. Chuck explained that the company had always been one where competition among managers was encouraged, though he had taken steps to mitigate competition since becoming CEO. "Being a very competitive place had its good points," Chuck said, "but we wasted time competing with one another instead of beating our competitors." At the same time, Chuck admitted that he subtly encouraged the competition to see how Barry would handle it. "I wanted to see him tested. Because if he made it, he'd have to manage these guys," Chuck explained. "And if he couldn't handle them now, he wouldn't if he became their boss."

Barry saw things differently. He faulted the organization structure that Chuck had created, and believed that Chuck should have done more to solidify Barry's position in the company. Because he remained an EVP, the new structure gave Barry a lot of power, but not as much as he wanted. Chuck had concentrated under Barry software development, new-product development in existing markets, finding and managing new alliances, commercialization of technologies for emerging markets, and a central project-management office for development projects that crossed unit lines. But Chuck had also consolidated several marketing departments and the company's sales forces, creating a large and powerful marketing/sales organization. To run it, he had created an EVP position for an ambitious and aggressive executive, George, who made it clear that he fully expected to be Chuck's successor.

Chuck made these changes for three reasons. The first was to reduce the number of people reporting directly to him. The organization structure had been flat: development, marketing, sales, and other related functions had reported directly to Chuck. This arrangement had enabled Chuck to keep a firm grip on each area while preventing any manager from forming a power base. It had worked well for the company, producing record volume and profits. It had also worked well for Chuck, who hadn't faced any threats to his power. But to prepare the organization for an era when he was no longer at the helm, Chuck believed that he had to create a smaller senior-level team.

The second reason for changing the organization structure was to increase the number of new products created through both internal development and alliances. Chuck saw a need to consolidate both initiatives under one person who could concentrate on the task. The third reason was to test Barry's ability to work successfully in a matrix-style organization, which Chuck viewed as the appropriate structure for the future. If Barry could perform well without direct control of marketing and sales, Chuck reasoned—that is, if Barry could influence George without the authority of a reporting relationship—he would demonstrate his ability to run the entire organization. Barry, however, was thinking more about what Chuck could do to make it easier for Barry to succeed in his current job. He believed that reaching his performance targets necessitated having under his control functions that reported to George.

Barry's View of His Situation

"I know I can do this job and deliver what the company needs," Barry told me about six months after joining the company. "But I've got one hand tied behind my back. George has an incentive for me not to succeed, because he wants the CEO job too. And if he doesn't make his sales targets, he can always say he didn't get the product on time from me." I asked Barry why he thought Chuck had structured the organization as he had. "I just think he doesn't get it. He's a smart guy, and he's been around, but he came up in a different time," he answered. "Today you just can't draw firm lines between the development of these products and their marketing and how they're sold. It's all one process, really, and to have two people at the same level over different parts of it just causes problems and slows things down."

I asked Barry if he thought that part of Chuck's motivation was to see if Barry could work well with someone who didn't report to him. "This isn't about relationships," Barry answered. "It's about how to get the best products into the market faster than our competitors. Anyway, I'm not real good at politics. I'm more comfortable with strategy. If I have what I need to get the job done, and I don't have to worry too much about the politics part, we can do great things here."

The chief financial officer recognized Barry's potential to benefit the company, and the hurdles that he had to overcome before it could be realized. She knew George well and recognized his abilities, but understood that his ambition and style could make collaboration with him very difficult. As a close adviser of Chuck's, she had participated in his decisions to hire Barry and to change the organization structure. When the new structure had been in place for a month or so, the CFO approached Barry to ask how things were going and to offer any help she could provide. She later described "a pretty brief conversation, pleasant enough, but it seemed like it surprised Barry a little, like he didn't know what to say." I asked if she thought he had failed to grasp what she meant and what help she could provide. "Probably something like that," she said. "Barry's world is pretty practical and tangible, and he probably was thinking he needs to get a couple of world-class software people in here and find the next great alliance that can give us some new products down the road. When I offered to help, I was talking about the relationship with George—and also with Chuck, because I could see Barry was struggling with the new structure. But I'm not even sure he sees the need to work on this relationship stuff."

Aware that the company made regular use of contractors, technical experts, and consultants, I asked Barry whether he had utilized any outside people. He mentioned product-development and technical experts, and added that he had organized "two technical advisory groups that are packed with some of the smartest people in the industry. That's one thing about Chuck, he really encourages you to find the smartest people you can find."

Barry has been at the company a bit more than a year. Chuck plans to retire in about twelve months. George has exceeded his targets and managed a diverse and geographically spread-out sales force. Barry too has achieved the objectives of the functions under his control. But release of new products has been slower than Chuck expected. The lack of a collaborative working relationship between Barry and George has hindered their people from working together. Barry may yet succeed Chuck, but that outcome is less certain than he had hoped it would be at this juncture. As a result, George is in a stronger competitive position than he otherwise would have been.

What Happened Here?

Barry has a blind spot when it comes to the political side of an organization. He does not recognize that relationships often determine the path of a career, especially at senior levels. That Chuck might view Barry's ability to handle a relationship with George as a succession test is a foreign idea to Barry. He believes that only tangible metrics should matter, like the number of new products delivered to the sales force or efficiency targets in cross-department projects.

Barry's second blind spot is that he is not attuned to how people perceive him and does not read their reactions accurately. He often misses what lies behind their questions and what they want of him. His rudimentary awareness of the impact of his own emotions on relationships and his low level of empathy also blind him to others' emotions.[2] This configuration affects how Barry listens and responds to people, which in turn determines the relationships he forms. His characteristic way of interacting with people is to propose a solution; Barry hardly ever responds reflectively or expresses empathy or supportiveness.[3]

But none of this rules out succeeding Chuck. Barry is very smart and self-confident. His high need for achievement and control, and high sense of self-worth, make him well suited to succeed at this company.[4] He also has a deep understanding of the products, the technology behind them, and the marketplace—all vital to his and the company's success. But if he is not chosen as Chuck's successor, the most likely reason will be his poor relationship-building skills. In order to improve his chances, Barry must make progress in three areas: (1) awareness of how his feelings and actions affect his relationships with other people, (2) anticipation of occasions when his emotions, rather than logic, are likely to affect how he behaves, and (3) his capacity to read how he comes across to other people. Chuck has talked to Barry about his shortcomings and urged him to find people who can help him. How can Barry find and apply the right advice? Let's look at what we know about how he approaches help. Two advice-related problems stand out.

Barry did not analyze his situation thoroughly enough. His logical skills led him to conclude that the organization structure hindered him from achieving what was expected of him. He was probably correct. But he failed to understand that first-rate operational performance, though important to the company, is only one of Chuck's objectives. The other is to test Barry's ability to work effectively in the style and structure he believes best suited to the company. Barry sized up his help needs one-dimensionally, just as he approached peer relationships.

Though Barry was quick to take advantage of the company practice of seeking the best help, the advisers he used were experts in technology, software development, program management, and venture/alliance analysis. None was skilled in the arena where he faced his biggest challenge: forming winning relationships and influencing without formal authority. Barry urgently needed help to understand the culture he hoped to lead and to grasp what it would take to become Chuck's successor. Perhaps his most promising source of help was the CFO. A close adviser to Barry's boss, she was influential in the company and very perceptive about relationships. She had reached out to Barry, but he had failed to grasp that she was offering help or that he needed the help she could provide. Nor had it registered on him that she would not have offered to help if she had believed that George was the best candidate to succeed Chuck. Not only was she in a position to help; she wanted Barry to succeed.

Sometimes success is elusive even in the presence of a comprehensive advice network if the leader fails to take full advantage of it. Consider the case of Wayne.

"I Know I'm Right"

Wayne was on a roll. He had been recruited to a household-products company after the chairman/CEO had set his retirement date. The chairman/CEO and the board had agreed that the next leader should be someone with energy, vision, and extraordinary sales and marketing abilities. The company had grown and prospered over the years by making dependable, high-quality household products. Revenues and profits had been solid and dependable. Shareholders could count on dividends; employees and their communities could count on steady jobs. It was a formula that had worked for years.

But an emerging generation of consumers who expected to move several times before settling permanently wanted less expensive products with multiple features rather than long-term dependability. And competitors were responding. The result for Wayne's new company was declining sales and market share. To increase sales volume, the CEO had reduced prices on the most popular (but low-margin) models, which had hurt profits. He had also maintained a respectable share price through an aggressive stock-buyback program. The combination had prevented the laissez-faire board from noticing a decline in market share. Several directors were friends of the CEO, and the board did not probe the strength of the company's performance or its core operating principles. The CEO insisted that there was no need for the radical steps competitors were taking, like closing U.S. plants or reinvesting profits rather than paying dividends, and the board agreed. Nothing fundamental needed to change; what was needed was better marketing. That's where Wayne came in. He had risen rapidly at a premier consumer-goods company, had set new records in each job he held, and was by far the most impressive candidate. If he could market the company as he marketed himself, the board reasoned, they had done their job.

Wayne joined as the number two with the understanding that, if things went well, he would become chairman and CEO when the chairman retired. The first couple of years did go well. Wayne's energy, leadership skills, and ability to sell his ideas were exactly what the company needed. He dissolved long-standing barriers between departments, promoted young people with new ideas, and hired managers with strong marketing and brand-management capabilities. Several new products had been in development before Wayne arrived, but his marketing, pricing, and product-positioning skills enhanced their success and revived the company's image and revenues.

Tensions with the Chairman

But there were tensions. The chairman had been unprepared for the emotional price he would pay for leaving a company where had spent his entire career, and the board had not done a good job of helping him cope with his personal transition. The chairman knew that the company's recent successes were Wayne's doing, but each time Wayne was given credit, the chairman felt hurt and envious. The two men remained distant. The board failed to see warning signs, but they were apparent to managers who interacted with both men. Some were loyal to the chairman; others believed in Wayne's vision for the company. As the chairman's retirement date approached, tension increased.

Wayne was more aware of tension than the chairman, and he had more at stake. But just as the chairman's pride had prevented him from reaching out to Wayne, Wayne's pride kept him from seeing to it that the chairman retired on a positive note. "Why should I bend over backwards to make things easier for him?" he asked. "Look at what I've done here in a few years. His stock is worth a lot more today than it was when I got here." Wayne also believed that he was inheriting a company that was less solid than it had appeared. The chairman, he said, "never invested much back into the business. He just kept things spinning and moving until he was ready to check out. It was financial engineering, not real value creation."

The chairman retired on schedule. Wayne immediately launched several initiatives, including a creativity/innovation program and an energetic pursuit of alliances to secure new technology. He initiated a company-wide productivity program to reduce costs and pay for new product-creation initiatives, and began to look into moving one of the company's plants overseas. Wayne also took personal responsibility for a foreign joint-venture project begun by his predecessor. Each of these efforts had potential to generate profitable growth in the future, but each also required capital, resources, and Wayne's time and attention. Meanwhile, revenue and profits in the core business languished. Instead of implementing the planned stock-repurchase plan, he reinvested available cash. As a result, the stock price declined slightly. And a labor action by a local union at the plant being considered for relocation overseas drew the attention of the national media.

Overwork and Stress

The other problem confronting Wayne was that his vision of what the company should become, though exciting to his senior managers, required skills and expertise that few of them possessed. He had been warned by outside advisers that the talent he had inherited did not match his aspirations for the company. He understood their point and took advantage of retirements to bring in a few people with the necessary capabilities, but decided not to change the senior team radically to avoid looking like a new boss in a hurry to change the company. This decision meant that Wayne had to shoulder more responsibility himself than he would have with the right team in place. He often found himself suggesting solutions that his people should have come up with. And the few people with ample experience and talent were also stretched too thin, depriving Wayne of their regular counsel. He had no internal advisers who could offer new perspective, feedback, or options.

The toll on Wayne was invisible to most people. His high-energy style was unchanged at work, but his wife Cathy saw a change. He put in eighteen-hour days for three or four weeks at a time and then, she recalled, "he would just crash and sleep pretty much the whole weekend."

Sometimes Wayne fell silent, refusing to talk about work at all. This worried her: Wayne had always used Cathy as a sounding board, and she was his primary personal counselor. But she decided not to push Wayne to talk, reasoning that he probably just needed time to relax and sort things out, and that he would seek her out when he was ready.

The board was uneasy too. The directors had kept their distance during Wayne's first year, but several had recently expressed dismay about the flat stock price and adverse publicity regarding plant closings. They also complained that, because of Wayne's travel schedule, he was often unavailable when they tried to contact him. Wayne acknowledged the importance of managing the board, but devoted practically no time to it between board meetings. "I know a board member called and I just didn't get to returning it for a week. I need to be more careful about that," he said. "But, you know, I've got a million things to do and every one is more important than talking with him. When they call, it's usually on something that just isn't very important. They just don't understand the business. If it's a good idea, chances are we've already thought of it. But most of time it's not a good idea. It's just a waste of time."

A Showdown with the Board

Wayne was preparing for an upcoming board meeting when the lead director called to request a meeting the following day. Wayne answered that he was booked from 7:30 a.m. through dinner. "I'll be there at 7," the director said. "This won't take long." The director's message was a simple one: the board's confidence in Wayne had eroded, and to restore it Wayne had to change the way he operated. The directors wanted him to scale back the alliance/new-product initiative, postpone further study of an offshore plant, explore pushing off the international joint venture, and devote more of his time to the core business. Though margins were lower than in other product lines, the core products were what the company was best known for. Volume could still grow, the directors believed, if more advertising was devoted to them and prices were lowered. The lead director told Wayne to bring a plan for progress on these items to the next board meeting.

Wayne protested that his top team was solidly behind his strategy, and that the company's current direction was not exclusively Wayne's plan; it had been crafted by the whole senior management group. The lead director replied that complaints had reached the board—he would not say from whom—that Wayne had not been open to managers' input or willing to be influenced about the programs he had put in place. The directors had the impression, he said, that managers felt they were being sold on Wayne's views, and that Wayne was not receptive to their ideas, cautions, or disagreements. Wayne asked if all of the directors had agreed with the directives he had just been given. The lead director said they had. Wayne said it sounded as though they had met more than once on this matter; the lead director said they had talked several times. Wayne spent the day shocked and distracted. Not until that evening did he get angry that the board had met behind his back, intruded into decisions that were management's to make, and above all questioned his stewardship of the company. He and Cathy talked until early morning.

Over the next several days, Wayne contemplated his options. He was convinced that investing scarce resources in the core products would be a mistake over the long run, and that his strategy was the only way to avoid a long, slow, steady decline. If his plan, or something like it, were not implemented now, he believed, the company would eventually be acquired. He was also convinced that without adding real value the stock price could only be propped up temporarily, and that the only way to add real value was to develop new products for domestic markets, shift older products to foreign markets, and cut manufacturing costs for traditional products. He was certain he was right. Cathy had two questions. One was whether he should talk to a few of his senior managers and involve them in helping him respond. Wayne said that this was something he as chairman should handle. She also wondered aloud why the board was becoming so much more active now, and speculated about whether the ex-chairman was involved.

Wayne realized that the ex-chairman had probably been talking to the board, and hypothesized that it was he who had passed on negative comments, probably from some of the older managers who maintained contact with their former boss. The ex-chairman had been unhappy about handing over the company to Wayne, and had never been a fan of Wayne's new strategy. As Wayne thought about what the lead director had said, things began to fall into place. It was not the sort of thing that the board would come up with on its own. Wayne had been advised to replace some directors with people who would be loyal to him and share his vision. This had been one of the tasks he had intended to get to once the strategy was in place. He now faced a bigger problem: if he was correct about the involvement of the ex-chairman, he could be fighting for his job.

Wayne concluded that he needed to convince the board that his strategy was sound. Supremely confident of his salesmanship skills, he was certain he could make this sale. Wayne cleared his calendar and spent a week preparing for the board meeting. At Cathy's urging, he also called an old friend who had advised him when he first joined the company as CEO. Wayne brought him up to date on the events of the previous year, the promising alliances, and the push for new products. Then he described the meeting with the lead director and what he intended to say at the next day's board meeting. His friend asked why Wayne thought the board would endorse a plan now that it hadn't previously supported, and pointed out that the lead director had requested a plan to change direction, not a presentation to convince them that Wayne's existing plan was the right one. Wayne felt himself becoming annoyed at being questioned. The real problem, he replied, was that he had never taken the time to fully explain his strategy to the board, and that once he did so they'd realize that his plan was best. "I hope that's right," his friend replied, "but what if you're wrong?"

"I'm not wrong," Wayne retorted. "They know they need me running this organization, and it won't look good for the new CEO to leave. Once I lay this out, they'll see I'm right."

Wayne's resignation was announced after the board meeting. He had done a very good job, the board said, but had resigned to pursue entrepreneurial opportunities and spend more time with his family.

What Happened Here?

Wayne's strategic mistake was to try to do too much too quickly without certainty that the core business units were in solid operating shape and could produce the profit necessary to support expansion. Wayne's workload and the time available to handle it were at odds. His senior team did not have the talent or experience necessary to execute Wayne's plan. He clearly took on too much, but his overreaching was exacerbated by the absence of a staffing structure suited to his style and shaped to his strengths and shortcomings. As a result, Wayne was left on his own to prepare for meetings and ensure follow-up of decisions. Sometimes decisions reached him prematurely, and he found himself asking people to return to him when they had more data or analysis. The net effect was insufficient time to concentrate on his A-item strategic priorities or on building relationships with directors.

Wayne's most serious mistake was political: he never fully gained control of the board as chairman. He had never run the board of a public company and had much to learn about managing board members. At the same time, the board and Wayne's predecessor bear much of the responsibility for a succession gone bad. Neither helped Wayne grab hold of the chairman's role or provided counsel after he did. But regardless of their culpability, Wayne was the one with the most to gain or lose. Had he made different decisions, the outcome would have been different.

Wayne missed a chance to install his own people on the board and failed to educate the directors he had inherited. He motivated people well and won the loyalty of both long-term employees and younger people new to the company; most lined up behind Wayne and were captivated by his vision. But he neglected to win over the directors in the same way. Because he had not recruited them, he felt little responsibility to manage board members or to make sure they were involved. His considerable energy was focused on the people under him and on running the company, not the board. In the final analysis, Wayne thought of himself more as a CEO than as a chairman.

Wayne neglected to build the sort of relationship with his predecessor that could have helped him with the board. He knew that the most powerful directors had high regard for the ex-CEO, and that his predecessor could help him build a positive relationship with them. But he did not seek out help or even ask for advice on how to build such a relationship. He let pride get in the way, convincing himself that he didn't need help to control the board. If Wayne had done so successfully, would the problem with the board have been avoided? Perhaps not. But ignoring the ex-CEO almost guaranteed resentment and a higher likelihood of political mischief. Wayne had had nothing to lose by trying to enlist the ex-CEO as part of his advice network.

Neither the board nor Wayne's predecessor helped him, but they did not stop him from getting the help he needed. Wayne's decisions about use of time and the initiatives he took on were his alone. Overconfidence was perhaps the most fundamental cause of his downfall. Sometimes an "I know I'm right" attitude affects how a leader treats his most trusted subordinates and how he handles their advice. If he doesn't do it well, the consequences can affect not only his relationships but also the future of the company. Consider what happened with Fred.

"My Managers Will Just Have to Crank It Up a Notch"

Fred had recently taken over a large and well-known but struggling consumer packaged-goods company. A highly regarded industry pro, he had worked for several large corporations and had twice been a president and CEO. He had introduced new brands that became industry leaders and revitalized others that had seen better days. But Fred privately believed himself more capable than the people to whom he had reported, and he wanted to prove his true worth before retiring. Offered the position of chairman and CEO by a board anxious for the company to be known again as an innovator and a good place in which to invest, he jumped at the chance. He lured high-quality talent from more successful competitors through personal salesmanship and the promise of financial reward from a turnaround. Soon he had constructed a team of some of the best people in the business.

Fred pushed his people hard, demanding flawless work, rigorous analysis, and no repeated mistakes. But he did not expect them to do anything he did not do himself, and he prided himself on his energy, hard work, and attention to detail. This style often created tension, which Fred had learned over the years to deflect with humor. He managed to keep the atmosphere from getting too tense, and kept his top team intact through the most difficult months of the turnaround.

After eighteen months, Fred's plan was ahead of schedule. He had secured new favorable financing and improved relationships with several large retailers that had cut back the company's shelf space and access to prime locations because of past poor service and inflexible pricing. Fred convinced them to position his products more favorably by promising better service and, eventually, exciting new products.

A Unilateral Decision

Fred made it known that he wanted to acquire new product lines. His success with retailers had convinced him that the time was right for such a step. To secure the support of people on his team who might consider it too early in the turnaround process to take on new product lines, he pushed the board's compensation committee to award the senior group restricted stock; he hoped this incentive would lessen their hesitations. In fact, Fred already had his sights set on something more ambitious than acquiring products: he had learned that a company about half the size of his would be open to acquisition. He hadn't contemplated buying an entire company, and certainly not such a large one, but the more he thought about it, the more excited he became. Fred saw synergistic opportunities in an integrated product line, and the sale of product lines that did not fit would generate money to reinvest in marketing and margin support to give him more pricing flexibility with retailers. It would be a big step while still in turnaround mode, but Fred believed it was the right thing to do.

It was more important than ever for the top team to be behind him. Fred scheduled an off-site on the topic of strategy, the first such session at the company. The offsite was held at a seaside resort, and the first half-day was devoted to golf and fishing. At dinner that night, Fred staged a roast of each team member. The tone was convivial, and the stage was set for productive work.

If Fred was convinced that the company could handle an acquisition, his CFO wasn't. He had worked for Fred at another company and was now Fred's closest internal adviser. Fred had asked him to examine the other company's numbers to estimate integration costs and synergy benefits. The CFO argued that the timing was wrong for an acquisition: the company's information-technology and financial systems wouldn't yet support an organization 50 percent larger, and the culture that Fred was building was just starting to jell. The CFO worried that an acquisition would arrest progress, and, worse, that the fragile infrastructure would crack under the load. As persuasive as the CFO's arguments were, Fred would not budge. He saw the acquisition as an opportunity that could not be passed up; the organization would just have to work harder, and the managers would have to crank it up a notch. Fred contacted the chairman of the other company and hired an investment bank.

The CFO had also opposed announcing the acquisition attempt at an off-site. He argued that Fred should talk to each senior manager individually, and solicit their views on the pluses and minuses of the acquisition. They would speak more freely in private, the CFO said, than at a meeting with their peers. Again, Fred disagreed. Given their travel schedules, individual meetings with his senior people would consume several weeks, raising the risk that word of a possible acquisition would leak out. At an off-site Fred could control the timing, and the announcement could be coordinated with their return.

A Stunned Response

At the end of the second day of the off-site, after a productive work session, Fred introduced the topic of the acquisition. The initial reaction to his announcement was silence. Fred filled the vacuum by describing how the two companies' products would fit together in the marketplace and even speculating about which plants might close and how the combined company would be organized. The more he talked, the quieter his listeners became. Most remained expressionless and avoided eye contact with Fred. Fred finally stopped talking and waited from someone to speak. After a full minute of awkward silence, the HR head suggested letting Fred's announcement sink in a bit. They could discuss it further, he said, at dinner that evening. Everyone seemed relieved and the meeting ended. People left the meeting room in pairs, talking in low tones.

At dinner, the first to speak was the head of marketing, a favorite of Fred's and a strong candidate to be his backup. Diplomatically, he credited Fred's leadership for bringing the company to a strong enough position to even consider a step that would have been inconceivable just six months earlier. Fred protested (partly out of conviction and partly for motivational effect) that it was the team around the table that had brought the company to this point. Then he joked that the marketing director's words were a preamble to "But the problem is . . ." No one laughed. The marketing VP said he was worried that an acquisition was too big a step and that the company was not ready. The plans for the next year were filled with tough goals, he said, and every department would have to work harder than ever just to achieve what had been committed to.

The HR VP pointed out that the prevailing stress level could lead to burnout and turnover. Others concurred. Fred did not argue or try to convince them of the deal's value; he was pleased that they were articulating their reactions, but sensed that something was still being withheld. He decided not to push the point and instead asked the CFO to describe what he had learned in his preliminary investigation. The CFO did so in his typical dry, factual way; Fred had hoped he'd express more enthusiasm. As dinner ended, Fred was pleased that the acquisition was on the table but wondered about other reactions that had not been revealed.

Early the next morning, the HR head asked to meet with Fred before the team reconvened. He told Fred that the group had gone to the hotel bar after dinner and stayed late talking about the organization's readiness for an acquisition. Their overriding feeling was anger that Fred had already hired a banker and started due diligence without their involvement. The heads of marketing, sales, and manufacturing—the departments that would experience the most pressure—had been particularly vocal. The HR head recommended that Fred tell the group that he understood the qualms they had voiced the day before and that he was anxious to hear any further misgivings they might have.

Fred took the HR head's advice. The first issue raised was the organization's readiness for an acquisition. The entire meeting was taken up with this topic and what would have to happen if the deal went through. Anger about exclusion from the decision went unmentioned. Fred concluded that the HR head had overstated people's anger or that the previous evening's discussion had laid it to rest. The protest he had anticipated from people whose departments would have to work harder with no more resources to make the integration work did not materialize. Fred left the off-site satisfied that all of his objectives had been met. Optimism, a can-do attitude, and hard work had always been his winning formula. The next phase would not be easy, but he was sure it was the right step.

Operational Glitches and Defections

Six months later, the deal was closed. But the next year did not go as well as Fred had hoped. Operating performance in the core business deteriorated: sales targets were missed and plant productivity goals were not met. Service was a continual problem, and big retail customers were becoming restless again. To win the support of analysts, Fred had to set tough cost-savings goals for the consolidation of the two companies. He was also frustrated with the inability of the IT and financial systems to produce accurate forecasts or to provide a timely enough picture of the state of the business to allow for prompt adjustments. Everyone, including Fred, was working longer hours than ever before, at a growing cost in illness, stress, and turnover.

The first to resign was the head of manufacturing, whose candor Fred had always counted on. Before his departure, he told Fred that the decision not to involve the senior team in the acquisition until the eleventh hour was a mistake that the team had never recovered from. Fred replied that people would have forgotten all about being left out if the integration had gone more smoothly. "Maybe so," the VP responded, "but it didn't go smoothly." Fred had underestimated the team's dismay, he indicated, just as he had underestimated what it would take for the integration to succeed.

The head of sales left a few months later, angry that Fred was still maintaining two separate sales forces. With no other viable option, Fred assigned sales to the head of marketing. The head of IT was next. He had decided to return to the larger, more sophisticated company Fred had hired him away from. He believed in Fred's vision, he said, but the building blocks to produce the systems and processes the company needed were simply lacking. He had enjoyed working for Fred and believed that his stock options and restricted stock would eventually have paid off, but he no longer believed he could do the kind of job that he and Fred both expected. The team that Fred had felt so good about just a year earlier had broken apart.

Two and a half years after the acquisition, the two companies were still learning to work together. IT systems remained problematic, and service levels were improved but still inadequate. A prime competitor approached Fred about buying the company. The stock had not grown as fast as Fred had hoped, and selling was the best deal for shareholders. Certain that the company's problems would be solved, Fred did not want to sell but understood his fiscal responsibility to investors. The sale went forward quickly. The company's name and several of its brand names disappeared when it was absorbed.

What Happened Here?

Did Fred's story have to end this way? Perhaps it did: the company had been poorly managed for years before Fred arrived, and much had to be fixed before its promise could be fulfilled. The acquiring company had the money, expertise, and management depth to do what was needed. On the other hand, the company did not need to be sold at that particular juncture. Fred had anticipated a sale at some point, to generate cash to increase market share and make acquisitions and to create wealth for himself and others. But he had envisioned such a step five or six years in the future, at a much higher sale price. In retrospect, if Fred had intended to sell when he did, the acquisition he made was probably unnecessary. And without the attendant distraction and pressure, profitability would almost certainly have been higher, leading to a higher sale price.

Fred's story may simply portray a leader who overextended himself and was opportunistic when he should have been conservative. It could even be argued that Fred and his team took over a troubled company and managed to produce a good return for investors. Either case is valid from a business point of view. But from a leadership and advice-taking point of view, one comes to a different conclusion. Fred underestimated the difficulty of implementing his integration plan. In particular, he misjudged the reactions of his top team and the depth of their anger about being excluded. Fred is an accomplished businessman and a good leader who has had many more successes than failures. Here he faltered, misreading the human and political aspects of the business challenge he faced.

But even after his first blunder, the advice he received from his two primary staff people could have helped him blunt its impact. The CFO's recommendation that Fred meet individually with members of the top team would have uncovered their indignation at being left out. Later, in an early-morning conversation at the off-site, the HR VP suggested inviting the team to air their grievances. Fred took the HR VP's advice but did not follow through, allowing the conversation to sidestep people's anger.

Would the outcome have been different if Fred had listened to his internal advisers? Probably. After all, they did not oppose the acquisition; they simply warned that the organization was unready. If Fred had probed, their reasons for reluctance might have made him more cautious, or prompted him to accelerate the steps necessary to achieve readiness. Another question is where the responsibility lies: did Fred discount the advice he received or did his advisers do a tentative job of expressing their reservations? In my experience, the answer is usually that both could have done a better job. But it behooves the leader to make sure he understands his advisers' reasoning. Fred had made up his mind before giving his people a chance to voice their worries. There had been nothing fatally wrong with his behavior up to the point when he informed them of his intent. At that point he should have slowed the pace enough to let his announcement sink in, and then should have listened carefully to his team's misgivings.

Five Capable Leaders' Mistakes: Underlying Causes and Practical Lessons

We've looked at five sets of not-uncommon missteps in the management of advice. Each of the protagonists is an accomplished leader with a record of hard work, skillful problem solving, and results-oriented management. But all stumbled into advice-taking traps that hindered them from achieving goals that were well within their reach. To understand why, let's look at the mistakes each one made and the underlying reasons why they happened.

Dave: Don't Make Up Your Mind Prematurely

Dave decided to leave a company where he knew how to succeed to enter unfamiliar territory where the rules were different. It took time for him to understand the culture and the managers' working style, time that should have been devoted to pursuing his ultimate objective: to become a chairman and CEO earlier than he otherwise would have. Had he paid attention to how his three advisers viewed him, and their questions about the culture he was about to enter, he would have understood the risks and key success factors better. His decision might have been the same, but he would have prepared for the new environment and almost certainly would have gotten off to a better start.

Two warning signs that Dave ignored were the unrealistic promises of his soon-to-be boss and his own responses to them. His desire for a particular outcome blinded him to the reality that he was in a negotiating situation: the chairman was selling the opportunity that he had correctly perceived Dave wanted most. But three people who knew Dave well expressed reservations that proved to be prescient. One was his wife. Why didn't Dave delve more deeply into her mistrust of his prospective new boss? The HR director of Dave's former company may have hit on the answer. When he pointed out the potential mismatch with the culture of the new company, Dave dismissed his observations. "I though at first that he didn't understand what I was saying," the HR VP recalled. "But I think that Dave wanted this, and really didn't want to look at a lot of reasons why it might not work."

Dave violated the first rule of great advice taking: keep an open mind and pay close attention when people who may be more objective than you offer advice. Make sure you grasp fully what they have perceived that you have overlooked. Maintaining an open mind requires being honest with yourself about why you want to pursue a particular path.

Rita: Don't Forgo Advice Because Others Might Fault You for Seeking Help

Rita is not at risk of losing her position because of mistakes and missed opportunities in her first year as CEO. But her loss of credibility with her managers will take time to regain, distracting her and her team. Also, the lost acquisition will give a competitor an advantage that could come back to haunt Rita's company. Rita's faulty decision to pursue an acquisition without the help of her managers was a missed opportunity to acquire new technology. It may also have provoked insubordinate behavior on the part of the VP of manufacturing during a discussion of productivity. The nagging credibility problem will be difficult for Rita to resolve.

Unlike Dave, Rita reached out for help by looking for new directors and calling her business-school professor. But she made a mistake typical of poor advice takers by selecting advisers (board members and graduate students) who were neither skilled nor experienced enough to help. Rita's poor choices of help could be attributed to her father's suspicion of outsiders. But Rita's decisions were motivated more by fear that her most senior subordinates would view reliance on help as a weakness. Rita violated the second rule of advice taking: never make an important decision on the basis of how it might affect your status in others' eyes. Doing so leads to misreading or underestimating what it takes to succeed. The best advice takers understand that it is more harmful to their status to fail single-handedly at something that could have succeeded with wise use of available help.

Barry: Don't Limit Your Advice Network to Your Comfort Zone

By failing to see his situation and its demands as clearly as others did, Barry may have unnecessarily helped a political competitor and given his boss reason to question whether Barry was the right successor. The CFO read the situation accurately and offered her help, but because Barry hadn't diagnosed his needs and deficits accurately, he passed up the opportunity to enlist her as an adviser.

The warning sign for Barry was his insistence that managing the political side of the company was less important than the technical requirements of his job. He defined "the politics part" as a distraction irrelevant to the challenges he faced. What he overlooked was that, at his level, technical or functional expertise is a given. The people who make it to the top and thrive there are sensitive to the political realities of their situations and see them as a necessity of organizational life. Barry's obliviousness to the importance of positive working relationships at the most senior levels caused him to misread the culture of his company and his boss's expectations. This blind spot caused Barry to misunderstand what was necessary to win the top job, and in turn to misjudge the type of help necessary for him to succeed. Barry violated the third rule of advice taking: put together a balanced advice network. Avoid overrelying on the types of advice you feel most comfortable with at the expense of help mastering new abilities.

Wayne: Don't Let Pride Get in the Way

Wayne's miscalculations, unlike those of the other leaders, cost him his job. He managed his time and priorities poorly, and tried to accomplish too much without putting in place what was required for success. He also ignored the one group that exercised power over his fate: the board. It is unclear whether the previous chairman was implicated in the board's decision, but Wayne's neglect of the board had left a leadership void. With an effort to influence and educate the directors, Wayne probably could have won their understanding and support of his goals for the company.

The warning sign for Wayne was his conviction that, because his way was best, others would fall in line in support. His analysis of the company's strategic weaknesses was accurate, and his prescription was probably sound. But he lost sight of the most important constituency, the board. Wayne treated the board as a subordinate rather than a partner. Given the situation he inherited, the directors' lack of sophistication, and the jealousy of the ex-chairman, any leader would have been hard-pressed to win over all the directors to a new, change-oriented agenda. But Wayne's lack of an advice network, internal or external, meant that he had no early-warning system to help him anticipate when to shift his attention or revise his use of time. Thus he utterly failed to detect problems that ended up becoming fatal.

Wayne's wife—his primary source of personal support—understood him better than anyone. But when his hectic pace began taking a personal toll, and he needed her counsel more than ever, he did not seek it. Perhaps he was still sorting out the issues; perhaps, as Cathy concluded, he just needed time to relax. But it was a mistake for Wayne not to talk to her until after the meeting with the lead director. It was also a mistake on Cathy's part to not reach out to Wayne. She knew that talking things through was his characteristic way of resolving troubling questions. Contemplating his options alone was not going to lead to the right plan of action; he needed to talk more than he needed to relax.

Why didn't Wayne seek out Cathy? "I was dealing with some very complex strategy problems," he said later, "trying to close a couple of complicated deals. And on top of all that, we had this local [union] in one of the plants stirring things up. These kinds of things I didn't ordinarily bring home with me." What Wayne overlooked was that these and other problems were affecting his judgment. The potential value of going over them with his wife was not to solicit answers but (1) to hear himself talk and perhaps reach some decisions, and (2) to reveal the pressure he was under, which would have enabled Cathy to point out that solutions eluded him because stress was undermining his ability to think in a clear-headed way.

Wayne's fatal mistake may have been that when he needed advice most—when the board began signaling that it was unhappy, well before it coalesced against him—he turned inward. He had access to trusted people both inside and outside the company who knew his decision-making style, but he did not utilize them when he needed them most. Why? His rationale for not confiding more in his wife—that he was grappling with technical and strategic issues, not political or personal ones— may be only part of the reason that he avoided talking to her. The other part might be embarrassment that the board had been meeting without him and that the situation had deteriorated to the point of a confrontation. Wayne violated the fourth rule of advice taking: when help is available, use it. Don't allow either pride or shame to get in the way.

Fred: Pay Attention to the Advice of Those Whose Support You Need to Achieve Your Goals

Fred jumped at an opportunity to acquire a competitor that increased the volume of his company by 50 percent and added valuable brands. But by doing so he caused the strategy he had put in place to spin out of control. The resulting stress caused the top team he had assembled to disintegrate, and opened the door for Fred's company to be bought prematurely. Fred had ignored the advice of his senior managers about the acquisition even though it was they who would have had to manage the integration. They also understood better than he did the capacity of the company to change.

Fred was so driven to prove he could grow his company quickly that he failed to grasp that his managers were handling as much as they could. He overestimated his own ability to extract more from them. As a result, he committed to a path too quickly and then refused to rethink it or adjust his direction. Turning his company into a powerhouse may have become more to him than a commitment to the shareholders and the business; it may have become a burning personal desire. He may have viewed the acquisition as the quickest way to reach his personal dream of retiring as an admired CEO of a large, well-known company. It was clearly so important to him that he embarked on a risky path without securing the support and commitment of his managers. Fred violated the fifth rule of advice taking: when a goal is so important that you are willing to risk a lot to achieve it, pay particular heed to the advice of people whose support you need.

What happened to Dave, Rita, Barry, Wayne, and Fred is all too common among leaders who seek to change their organizations in some fundamental way. The changes that all five leaders pursued would have improved their companies. None of them was a poor leader. These competent, able leaders all lacked a conceptual vocabulary for thinking about their advice needs. And that deficit caused them to ignore warning signs and to fall into traps that seriously compromised their change agendas, even though advice was available that could have prevented their missteps. Necessary changes, capable leaders, available help—what was missing? There were at least four missing pieces:

- Core principles on which to build a model for great advice taking.

- A framework of roles, rules, and norms on which to base a search for appropriate advisers and optimal use of the advice they offer.

- A model of attributes and abilities that distinguish leaders who are good at using advice from those who are not.

- An understanding of the key success factors that can help turn general principles and attributes into applicable tools.

Chapter 3 will offer a framework of precisely the kind that these five leaders needed to guide them in the task of finding and using the right advice.

CHAPTER **3**

A New Framework for Advice Taking

AVOIDING THE PITFALLS that ensnared the five leaders introduced in chapter 2 starts with some systematic thinking about advice, which is the first step in a quest for a more comprehensive theory of advice taking. This chapter will begin that quest by briefly introducing a set of *fundamental principles* and a *framework* for differentiating between various types of advice and kinds of advisers. We will then look at the *attributes* and skills of wise advice takers—those who get the most from the help available to them—and *success factors* that are the key to making the most of useful help. The remainder of the chapter will delve into the fundamental principles more deeply, and subsequent chapters will deal with the other three components in detail.

Fundamental Principles of Advice Taking

Successful advice taking is founded on four fundamental principles:

- The leader's needs should determine both the content of the advice he receives and the nature of the relationship between leader and adviser. Advisers should adapt the help they provide to the leader's style and to the situation he faces, always viewing their own role and contribution from the advice taker's point of view.

- Different challenges call for different types of advice and different kinds of advisers. It is the leader's responsibility to understand his needs well enough to choose among the various kinds of help available. It is then up to the leader to manage his relationships with advisers to ensure that he received what he needs in the most actionable way.

- Opinions of the leader on the part of followers, bosses, and other stakeholders—a key component of the leader's credibility—will be enhanced by wise and skillful use of advice.

- In the most challenging leadership situations, the issues facing the leader have different impacts on success. The most problematic are political or personal in nature, and the right advice is particularly indispensable in these spheres.

We will examine these basic principles in considerable detail later in the chapter, after an orientation to types of advice and kinds of advisers, and to the attributes characteristic of skilled advice takers.

Types of Advice

When facing complex challenges, a leader cannot afford to depend on a single type of advice, or only one adviser. The types of advice available to a leader facing the tough challenges of a change agenda correspond to the kinds of needs these leaders experience:

- *Strategic* needs having to do with the direction of the enterprise and the broad choices that will equip it best to thrive.

- *Operational* needs pertaining to how the enterprise operates day to day and the processes and systems it depends on for routine forward motion in the most cost-efficient way.

- *Political* needs involving the nature of interpersonal relationships, internal competition for influence, and the interplay of coalitions and interest groups.

- *Personal* needs having to do with the leader's emotional requirements, tolerance for stress, and ability to stay on an even keel in
  the face of pressure.

Given the strikingly different natures of these four realms, expecting
a specialist in one area to offer comparably useful help in another is
roughly equivalent to expecting an oncologist to be as expert at treating
infectious diseases as he is at understanding the progress of a particular
cancer in one patient. Wise advice takers recognize the unique requirements of each sphere and tailor their expectations and management of
each specialist accordingly.

Kinds of Advisers

Advisers differ in how they are equipped to offer advice. But the focus of
their attention and capabilities is not the only way in which they differ.
Different advisers also play different roles in the leader's efforts to improve his organization, and therefore form different relationships with
the leader. Four advisory roles each fill a specific need for the leader pursuing a new agenda.

Experts offer deep, specialized knowledge to leaders who seek greater
understanding of or help implementing strategic options, operational
tools and techniques, or change in the culture of the organization. They
are steeped in the history and varied approaches of their fields, sometimes fortified by academic degrees and/or long experience of trial and
error applying various theories.

Experienced advisers have themselves held a job like the leader's and
have confronted similar challenges. Sometimes the leader's predecessor
can serve as an experienced adviser. Alternatively, an experienced adviser who has led a similar organization also understands the leader's job
from the inside, with the added advantage of familiarity with conditions
the leader anticipates facing himself. Ideally, the experienced adviser has
run an organization that operated as the leader wants his organization to
operate.

Experts and experienced advisers both offer substantive knowledge
or wisdom that can fill gaps in the leader's understanding of what needs
to be done. The third kind of adviser shares some of their skills but makes

a different type of commitment. *Partners* often have expert credentials, but become more directly involved than other experts or experienced advisers in the leader's change efforts, signing on to provide continuous help of longer duration. This sustained involvement has several advantages: (1) A partner becomes more involved in implementing recommendations. (2) He gains a deeper understanding of the organization's potential and capacity to change, and of the leader's vision for the organization and her needs for help as she guides it there. (3) The adviser forms a strong relationship with the leader and with senior managers, board members, and other stakeholders important to the change effort. (4) A high level of involvement and familiarity enables the partner adviser to help the leader link and manage various types of advice. As an architect does for a client, the partner will clarify a master plan and advise the leader on marshaling and managing the resources to make it a reality.

Sounding-board advisers may or may not offer specialized knowledge or deep experience. What distinguishes them is that they offer a safe harbor where the leader can express what is on his mind and what he feels, secure in the knowledge that the conversation is confidential. The best sounding-board advisers listen actively and with understanding, enabling the leader to talk through his preoccupations and regain clarity about the path forward.

The basic framework of this approach to advice taking consists of three components: (1) four types of advice, each matched to a particular set of needs the leader faces; (2) four kinds of advisers, who play different roles as the leader confronts the challenges of succeeding in his position and improving the organization; and (3) the leader's need for a balanced advice network that provides the right types of advice and the right kinds of advisers.

The Attributes of Skilled Advice Takers

Because he has the most to gain or lose, it is up to the leader more than the adviser to make the most of the advice available to him. This is why the attributes demonstrated by expert advice takers largely have to do with what they believe and how they behave. Skilled advice takers view help as necessary to achieving what they are after, and as a result are open to new ideas and feedback. This stance often goes hand in hand with a commitment to self-awareness, and willingness to take personal responsibility for managing the changes needed to realize a new vision.

These beliefs are expressed in a set of behaviors that are far more characteristic of expert advice takers than of those who are less effective:

- Skilled advice takers are deliberate in choosing the best type of help and in constructing a network of advisers.

- They manage that network actively, putting it high on their list of priorities.

- They work at building good relationships. To derive the most help from their advisers, they understand that they must take feedback without becoming defensive and, above all, listen with understanding.

- They seek advice and counsel quickly when faced with situations that can affect their plans. They also involve their advisers early in anticipating hindrances.

Key Success Factors

The final building block is a set of keys to success in making the best use of the framework and mastering effective advice taking:

- Find advisers before you face the problems that require their skills. Then build relationships with them so that their advice will be available when needed.

- Give your advisers access to you—to your schedule and your thinking—so that they can understand your style and the demands on you.

- Don't expect the adviser to do your job. Only you can generate an image of the ideal culture, decide on the elements that most need to be changed, or decide how to define success.

If these principles appear to represent common sense rather than blinding insight, it is because clarity often reveals itself only in hindsight. In addition to making the obvious explicit, their value arises from synergy: in combination, they acquire more power.

A Closer Look at the
Fundamental Principles of Advice

Advice Should Be Tailored to the Advice-Taker's Point of View

To be optimally helpful to the advice taker, both the content of advice and the way it is offered must primarily meet his unique needs, not those of the adviser. Skilled advisers customize what they do to the style and situation of each leader they advise. This does not mean that they change chameleonlike for each new client. It means that they tailor their approach to the leader's style, situation, and preferences to maximize his grasp of the help being offered and to ensure that it is in the form that he can use most easily. Average advisers, on the other hand, proceed more or less identically regardless of the leader's style or situation and simply expect the leader to adapt.

Advisers whose approach is leader-centered begin by carefully getting to know the leader's situation, how she views the needs and demands she faces, and her interpersonal, influence, learning, and decision-making styles. This discovery process usually begins with listening to how the leader sizes up her situation and has come to understand the problems or opportunities she faces. Has she considered the subjective, less concrete aspect as well as the tangible, objective part? Has she clearly grasped the risks and potential rewards? Is she aware of the political realities of his situation? Does she recognize what she does not know but needs to know? Is she asking the right questions?

FIGURE 3-1

Fundamental principles of advice taking

- The nature and delivery of advice should be defined from the point of view of the advice taker.
- Different challenges call for different kinds of help.
- The right help managed well enhances the leader's image.
- At senior levels, political and personal issues require the most help.

Throughout this situational analysis, the adviser will be taking the measure of the leader. This process resembles the due diligence undertaken by a company seeking a fuller understanding of another company it wants to acquire. The adviser asks himself: How self-aware is she? Does she understand how she comes across to others and the impact they in turn have on her? Is she aware of her emotions as she experiences them? How mature and emotionally secure is she? Does preoccupation with image or status compel her to get involved where others could do a better job? Does she have to have the last word in a conversation? Does she go out of her way to point out her accomplishments? Does she listen more than she talks? Does she observe people well and read their emotions accurately?

Meanwhile, the adviser is also exploring the leader's preferred way of making decisions. Is she comfortable choosing among options or does she prefer to be offered one well-thought-through position? If she wants options, does she prefer that they be presented early or after they have been vetted? Some leaders prefer to receive the adviser's thoughts in writing and to prepare a response, while others gain more insight from open-ended discussion with little preparation. Some leaders figure out what to do by talking through the options with someone they trust. Others are more comfortable deliberating alone. This may be the right time for the leader to volunteer what she considers her ideal way of receiving information and how she learns best. Ideally, the adviser should raise these questions before the leader does; in any case, it should raise a red flag if the leader brings up these matters and the adviser reacts as if he has never thought about them before.

Decision-making and learning styles are preferences developed over decades. Can they change? This is a relevant question for the leader of a successful organization who seeks to alter how it functions. While asking others to change, must the leader also look at how he himself operates? The answer is "Yes, but . . ." The leader should not be exempt from upgrading his leadership abilities. But by the time someone is leading an organization, his decision-making, learning, interpersonal, and influence styles have been in place a long time. He will not change easily or quickly, and wise advisers will not try to get him to do so. Instead they might take a two-phase approach. First they might look for ways to supplement or shore up how the leader operates, ranging from relatively simple (altering when the leader enters the decision-making process) to moderate (putting in place a senior staff aide) to dramatic (reorganizing the top team and replacing senior managers). Then they might give the leader feedback and counsel over time to reorient how he makes decision, deals with those around him, and the like.

If the relationship is defined from the adviser's point of view, by contrast, the leader must adapt to the service the adviser is offering rather than the reverse. The leader can end up feeling like a customer at a car dealership who discovers that the manufacturing and distribution system does not operate in his favor. The manufacturer offers many options to satisfy a wide range of needs and preferences, but the customer ends up settling for more or different features than he wants because they are part of the package. The consumer is forced to conform to the manufacturer's needs for efficiency in design, production, and inventory control because it is unrealistic to expect the carmaker to offer what the customer wants and no more. Helping a leader at times of upheaval, when the outcome affects the livelihoods of many people, should not resemble buying a car.

An apt analogy for help tailored to the leader's needs might be the actions of a skilled primary-care physician who schedules only the tests his tentative diagnosis indicates to be necessary and who factors in the patient's personal considerations and time constraints. Because the consequences of getting it wrong are serious, he inquires carefully about family history, lifestyle, tolerance for medication, and understanding of risks. He does not expect the patient to have sized up her own situation, but recognizes that the formation of a trusting relationship will encourage the patient to volunteer information necessary for a diagnosis and treatment plan. In an approach of this kind, focused on the recipient of help, the doctor adapts to the patient's needs as thoroughly as possible.

Similarly, a leader taking hold in a new job or changing established organizational patterns should not have to adapt to, or settle for, the particular consulting approaches or products that advisers offer. And adapting to the leader's needs is as much of an obligation for internal advisers as it is for external advisers. For example, the subordinates of a leader new to his position and hoping to become internal advisers should pursue a due-diligence process similar to that of the external adviser. They too must put themselves in his shoes to try to view the challenges of change from the leader's point of view.

Take the case of a new CEO who launched a companywide process-improvement effort combining Six Sigma discipline and a lean-enterprise mind-set. She emphasized greater responsiveness to customer complaints, better measurement of operations at every level, speedy decision making, and less time-consuming analysis. As she put it, the company had to "do half the analysis, make a decision, and then keep adjusting as we implement. We're losing customers because we're taking too long to respond." To direct the effort, she tapped a long-time senior manager, sacrificing experience in the new approaches for familiarity with and sensitivity to the organizational culture and political environment. Less than a year later, she replaced him, frustrated that education and pilot programs had not been put in place quickly enough. During a lessons-learned exercise it became apparent that the senior manager had never understood exactly what faster decision making or better measurement would look like. Though he worked hard at implementing new techniques, he continued to employ the style that was most comfortable for him. The CEO's mistake was assuming that the senior manager would understand what she meant. His mistake was allowing her to be less than crystal-clear about what she had in mind—that is, what she would see, hear, and feel when the organization was operating as she intended.

The effect of one's point of view on the helping relationship is illustrated by an experience I had years ago. Another consulting firm asked me to visit one of their clients. In the course of the consulting assignment, they had uncovered problems in our area of specialty. Though they could identify the problems, they could not implement solutions that would squarely address root causes. Rather than risk damaging a good relationship, they looked for someone who could supply what the client needed.

I went alone and met two people from the other firm: the consultant who directed the firm's work with this client, and his boss, an executive vice president responsible for growing the firm's market share with companies like this one. We began by meeting with the president of the company. The EVP took the lead, asking the president questions and occasionally mentioning further work his firm could perform. Eventually he suggested that he, the other consultant, and I meet to review his firm's analysis. I said that I would prefer to tour the plant to get a firsthand view of the situation the president had described. I asked the president to lead us, and he seemed pleased with the idea.

The tour took about two hours, as the president and I dug into details about new equipment that the company had had difficulty making productive, and the process- and product-quality program that he was unsatisfied with. He then agreed to an impromptu focus group, over lunch in the employee cafeteria, with several supervisors, hourly workers, and the plant manager. Afterward the president admitted that he spent little time in manufacturing and had just learned about some problems he hadn't known of before. At the end of the visit, the president asked how my firm might help. I said that because we had heard at lunch that his manufacturing people were committed to launching an improvement program, it would be best to see how that initiative panned out rather than introducing someone new from outside. Because the manufacturing people were quite powerful politically, and knew more about what they were facing than the president did, they would probably resist a solution that he imposed on them.

Returning to Boston with the consultant, I asked why his boss, the EVP, had seemed uneasy during the plant tour. He said that the EVP had asked, "Does Dan really know what he's doing? Why is he asking all those questions?" He recognized from my silence that I didn't understand what he meant. The EVP, he said, "was surprised that in the president's office you didn't make a presentation. You didn't describe Rath & Strong's work until the end of the day, and even then you only mentioned things you guys do that deal with the problem we were discussing. We're taught two things for a sales call. Impress them with how smart we are, and point out things we know that they don't but should. Then present what we do as early as possible, to make sure the client has our consulting product in mind when we're talking. You didn't do either one." He went on that the length of the tour was a surprise to the EVP, and that he was "very uncomfortable getting the supervisors and workers together without an agenda or preparation—and he couldn't understand when you turned down business and said you didn't think you could help."

What is the lesson of this story? There are different ways to help; what is best in one situation will not be appropriate for a leader facing something different. The other firm is very good at what it does, but when it came to needs outside their specialty, they were smart enough not to go too far down the path of trying to meet them. They are very good at laying out big, bold steps to a leader with broad strategy questions about how his organization can compete more effectively. This client needed that, but in order to make those steps work he also had to resolve some immediate problems embedded in day-to-day operational processes and complicated by a political climate in which powerful manufacturing managers resisted the involvement of anyone from the outside. The advice they had to offer was insufficient and they knew it. Putting the leader at the center of the helping relationship means that his needs shape the advice he receives. (We eventually did end up with the company as a client, but only after we spent more time with the manufacturing people and they initiated the request.)

Different Challenges Call for Different Kinds of Help

I have already used the physician–patient relationship several times as an analogy for the ideal leader–adviser relationship. There is another way the two relationships are analogous. As our knowledge has deepened about how the human body functions and reacts to stimuli, and as technology has opened new doors to understanding, medicine has become more and more specialized. As a result, the number of medical specialties and subspecialties has mushroomed. That different challenges require specialized types of help may seem so self-evident that it is not necessary to highlight it as a fundamental principle. But the reality is that most leaders do not use this principle to guide their advice-taking decisions. Instead they settle for help from people who are better suited to dealing with problems other than those the leader is facing. Here is an example.

A friend took over a struggling financial-services company. It soon became apparent to him that the company had serious systems problems because of out-of-date information technology and processing. He quickly brought in a consulting firm specializing in that area. By his six-month point, he had concluded that there were teamwork problems in addition to technical and procedural problems, especially when people had to work with others outside their own departments. Within individual departments, he had noticed, people responded to his calls for faster decision making and more teamwork, but they seemed incapable of either one when working with another department. His predecessor, through a hub-and-spoke management system, had dealt with each area separately and discouraged collaboration. But this new CEO's turnaround plan and his managerial style demanded interchangeability of people between units, frequent communication, and fast decision making, which in turn required sharing information and aiming toward common objectives. All of this represented a new way of operating for the company's managers. He correctly diagnosed his organization as having a culture that would retard his improvement strategy, if not scuttle it entirely.

Then he made his biggest mistake by asking consultants from the information systems consulting firm to add on a culture-change effort. A year later, things were worse. Though the information-systems consultants had used the same approaches that experts in the culture change might have, their lack of experience had caused them to ignore subtle factors that are important for success in that area. For example, a diagnosis of the culture was done, but it was introduced to employees in a way that raised suspicions rather than preparing the organization to be honest about problems. As a result, data were contradictory and analysis incomplete.

The consultants correctly pointed out that most upper- and midlevel managers, on whom the burden of the change effort rested, did not fully understand what the new CEO wanted them to do differently, though he had talked to them extensively and sent them memos and e-mails. Because they did not question him, he had assumed that they understood the problems as well as he did. He had pointed out, for example, that many "non-value-added" activities retarded fast responses to a rapidly changing marketplace. But these managers had run their departments in a particular way for years, and had been consistently rewarded for doing so. They were unsure which activities under their control added value and which did not, but were embarrassed or afraid to ask for clarification.

The consultants recommended a "vision-clarification" project—not a bad idea, except that they urged the CEO to explain in greater detail the long-range plan that he and the senior managers had formulated. At a series of time-consuming town-hall meetings, the CEO and CFO explained the markets that were to be penetrated, the financial benefits of doing so, and the need for the whole company to operate in a collaborative team-oriented way. Attendees filled out feedback forms after each meeting. Processed by the consulting firm and and presented to the CEO, they revealed ongoing uncertainty. One response was particularly striking to the CEO: "This meeting was helpful in going into more detail about the long-range plan. But I thought the objective of the meeting was to make it more clear what you wanted us to do more of and less of. I'm still not clear what you expect me to do differently—how I'm supposed to act that is different from how I act now."

What eluded both the CEO and the consulting firm is that a leader's vision is not the same as a long-range plan. The leader's vision of a changed state is the image in his mind's eye of how people will act once it has achieved what is in the long-range plan. It describes in vivid terms what will be visible that is not currently seen, what will be heard in meetings and conversations that is different from what one now hears, and what emotions will be felt that aren't currently prevalent.

For example, one problem at this company was slow response rates to customer complaints. The CEO's vision should spell out how the ideal future organization will respond when a dissatisfied customer calls. The company was also slow to respond to competitors' innovations; the vision should describe what one should see, hear, and feel when a competitor releases a new product with market-changing potential. Another problem was high turnover of new employees, especially in the first six months after being hired; the vision should clarify how the organization will recruit, hire, and orient new employees, how managers will be trained to assimilate them, and what will happen if they do not do a good job. It is in this way that the CEO can establish new standards for employees' behavior by clearly describing what he expects of them.

The point here is that even though the CEO and the consulting firm aimed in the right direction and often asked the right questions, they largely missed the mark, wasting valuable time, risking damage to the leader's credibility, and distancing him from the people he had to redirect. Why? Because the CEO assumed that advice is fungible and that advisers expert in one area can easily provide help in another.

The Right Help Enhances the Leader's Image

Many people worry that accepting advice will be seen as an admission that they do not have all the answers, and therefore as a sign of weakness. Every leader wants to appear decisive, in control, and in possession of what it takes to be in charge. The right image is important, because how people view a leader determines their willingness to follow. But followers' affiliation or defection is influenced by other factors besides the appearance of authority: whether the leader is spending time on the issues that are most important to them and to the long-term health of the organization, and whether the leader's decision making is careful, wise, and judicious. If followers believe the leader is falling short on these two measures, their willingness to be influenced will give way to wariness and skepticism. If they observe the leader seeking out others' points of view and doing whatever is necessary to make sound decisions on crucial issues, their trust and willingness to follow into unknown territory will be reinforced.

Use of help when it is needed is not an indication of weak leadership or poor decision making. A leader is much more likely to be judged ineffective for underestimating serious problems that could have been avoided or resolved with the right help. Subordinates, bosses, and boards will find it difficult to forgive the leader who shunned available help in an ill-fated attempt to do the job on his own. Just as we are judged by the company we keep, people's impressions of a leader in a new position, or at times of change, are enhanced by the choice of wise advisers with the right experience.

Some leaders reject advice because they fear that they will have to cede control of their prerogatives—that help will somehow tie their hands. What usually happens, though, is quite the opposite. A leader who follows an unfamiliar path alone, and is subject to unexpected forces, has less control than if she were accompanied by people who had traveled a similar path before. Rita is an example of a leader whose image was tarnished rather than enhanced because she chose to proceed on her own.

Tim is an example of a leader who realized that he couldn't succeed on his own and who found his image enhanced by how he managed advice. Tim took over a well-known not-for-profit institute after the death of its revered founder. Despite successful fundraising and programs, the organization was facing serious problems. For years the founder had not managed the organization tightly or controlled expenses. His charm and fundraising abilities had kept the organization afloat, often barely averting financial crisis. Perhaps because he could not face the reality of the situation or admit his role in creating it, the founder had kept the board in the dark about the state of the institute's finances. Not only did Tim succeed an icon; he inherited an organization needing radical restructuring but not knowing it.

Tim's first thirty days were rocky. He discovered that the prevailing ignorance of the organization's financial status was matched by the depth of its financial straits. Each successive meeting with the CFO, outside auditors, and key managers deepened his alarm. He delivered a frank report to the board of trustees. By his four-month anniversary, Tim had spent most of his time on the financial crisis and very little on the strategic and organizational questions that lay ahead of him: securing the next round of government grants while preparing the organization for a layoff and persuading it to embrace a more cost-conscious mentality. He also wanted to accomplish all this without pointing a finger at his predecessor.

Tim decided to schedule an off-site meeting with his direct reports followed by a town-hall meeting of the entire staff to lay out the extent of the problem. His objective for the off-site was to ensure that his vice presidents understood the seriousness of the situation and endorsed Tim's program to solve it. Because he was not sure how they would react, he scheduled the off-site in two segments a week apart. If his VPs resisted, he could use the interval to decide on an alternate path. The first segment confirmed Tim's fears: most of his senior staff tried to explain away Tim's analysis. "They were in denial, and it was going to take a lot to open their eyes," Tim recalled. "And because I was the new guy, they weren't going to believe it just because I said it."

Tim asked two people for help. One was a former trustee who had been a friend of the founder and an executor of his estate. The other had co-founded the institute with Tim's predecessor and had been its head of administration before retiring. Tim hoped that, because of their association with his predecessor and the regard in which they were held, they could lend influential support to his message. One of the two came to the second half of the off-site and helped convince Tim's managers of the existence of problems they all had a stake in solving. Both attended the town-hall meeting, an important show of support for Tim.

The turnaround called for some tough steps, including the first layoff in the organization's history, replacement of the CFO, and the forced retirement of a long-time senior vice president. But within a year Tim had reoriented the organization and installed a more disciplined management process while reducing operating expenses. In a report to the board eighteen months after his arrival, Tim credited two factors for the success of the turnaround. One was the new CFO, who had won the support of the institute's independent auditors and instilled a rigorous cost-management system. The other was the two advisers:

> *I wouldn't be here today if it weren't for their support. When I asked them to help me, to be honest, my rationale was more cosmetic than anything else. I wanted you and the auditors to believe I had these people on my side—that if they agreed to help me, you would support me more. In fact, I got more. Because they agreed to help me, I had more credibility than I could have won on my own at that point. I found I got two other things that were even more important. They were the ones who gave me perspective on this place that I would never have been able to understand on my own. And because of the tough messages I was sending, few of the people on my staff trusted me at first. They also kept me focused on the A-item priority of fixing the organization instead of getting distracted by my own needs. When I came here and found out how bad the financial situation was, I believed I had been misled, and I didn't know if I could trust you. I was so angry that I lost sight of why I came here. At one point, [one of the advisers] wrote me a note that I would like to read:*
>
>> *Tim, you have a choice. You can bitch and moan about the situation you are in. And, yes, you probably have a right to. But while it will release some anger now, in the long run it won't make you feel any better. The other thing you can do is pick yourself up, grab this thing with both hands, and fix it. You know as well as we do that, for all its problems, this organization does a great job and has tremendous potential to do more. If it goes down because of the management mistakes of the*

past, a lot of people who deserve more, who depend on the institute, will be hurt. That, in and of itself, makes what you're going through sort of an investment on their behalf.

Tim realized that he could not succeed on his own because, as a new leader, he had not yet established enough credibility for his tough recommendations to be accepted. He succeeded in large part because of the advisers he selected and his adept management of their help. He used the support of these admired people skillfully, setting up his off-site in such a way that he could invite one of them in if needed. Tim was open with both advisers about his expectations and worries. He kept them informed about his plans and made sure he was available to them whenever they wanted to reach him. Tim is a confident leader who can usually handle tough situations on his own. But in this situation he recognized that he needed help, and he never hesitated out of concern that using help would be seen as a weakness.

Other leaders need help when they get caught in a political web or become neutralized by the stress and pressures of being the person at the top.

Political and Personal Needs Call for the Most Help

Every leader finds that four kinds of needs demand time and attention: strategic, operational, political, and personal. But just as business problems have differential weight and urgency, so do the leader's needs. Some types of help are more crucial than others. For leaders who need to rally others' support for a change agenda, and to maintain personal balance and mental toughness in the face of unremitting stress, needs for help fall into two categories: important and essential.

Important Help: Strategic and Operational Needs

A well-equipped leader's *strategic* arsenal typically begins with an understanding of the organization's current course and the implications of maintaining it, along with comparable familiarity with alternative strategic courses. As he makes that assessment, he judges the capacity of the organization to change, innovate, and become more profitable. Also necessary is a solid grasp of what the organization seeks to achieve on behalf of, and what it requires from, its external stakeholders (customers, investors, communities, and suppliers) and internal stakeholders (employees and retirees).

Awareness of how competitors are seeking to meet the same needs—including what they do better and less well, and how they think about the same challenges and problems—is another piece of the strategic puzzle. And the leader must also ensure that the organization possesses a firm grasp of geopolitical, economic, and social forces that affect its future. Once he fits all the pieces together, he will engage senior managers and board members in crafting objectives and the strategy-level path that will achieve them. As he pursues these steps, he is clarifying the picture in his mind's eye of the new culture, including the types of people necessary to achieve what has been laid out.

Operational needs involve the organization's capabilities to operate efficiently day to day and to meet short- or mid-term targets on an ongoing basis. The components of these capabilities include design, installation, and evaluation of the tools and techniques that keep the organization working effectively (including information technology and financial reporting and control systems); processes to ensure product or service quality; standards for cost containment and budget control, and an efficient process to realize them; and maintenance of the human resources to keep the organization going (the mechanics of finding, motivating, rewarding, and separating employees).

Getting strategic and operational needs right is the core of any leader's job. On the strategic front, the destination that the organization aims at, the path to follow toward it, and the means employed to persuade the organization to follow should be initiated by the leader and no one else. Operationally, he must set the drumbeat to which the organization marches. It is also up to him to ensure that the march forward has the benefit of the right tools, processes, and support lines, and that they are managed as efficiently as possible.

Most people reach the top because they have mastered the management skills that strategic and operational challenges call for. And there are plenty of places to turn for help: management consulting and auditing firms specialize in one or both of them. But these are not, in the final analysis, the abilities that distinguish excellent from average leaders. And

when one's career is at stake and/or big change agendas must be implemented, strategic and operational skills are not enough. In such a situation, the leader's bedrock dependence on the support and perspective of
colleagues and subordinates, on conformance of the interests of coalitions and alliances with the leader's direction, and on his own personal
hardiness and resilience are crucial. It is for this reason that help with political and personal needs is most essential.

Essential Help: Political and Personal Needs

The *political* dimension of a leader's job has to do with the network of alliances and coalitions responsible for hindrances or for the intensity of
support for his agenda. It is also a matter of knowing who can be trusted
and to what degree, as well as who the people important to the leader's
success trust and why. If alliances and coalitions form the organization's
central nervous system, its heart is the organization's culture: why it is
important to employees, which of its features they value most, how core
values came to be and what sustains them, and the individuals who are
key to maintaining the culture or changing it. To effectively manage the
political part is to recognize and understand the shadow organization—
the pattern of relationships that accounts for how decisions are really
made and how things actually get done.[1] But the shadow organization
remains obscure to some leaders, typically because of the isolated perch
they occupy, their own lack of training and familiarity with political and
cultural matters, and their dependence on an information/communica-
tion system that shields them from bad news. Those who allow such iso-
lation inevitably lose the battle on the political front.

For a leader operating under the aegis of a powerful chairman or
board, or the leader of a division, political needs include building a relationship with the boss and/or the board and with influential peers. This
is a situation that typically calls for heightened "cue awareness"—accurate interpretation of the usually subtle indicators of key factors in success at this level in a particular culture. This is the aspect of politics that
tripped up both Dave and Barry, as we saw in chapter 2.

The second essential element is *personal.* For the person in charge
during a time of change, stress is an inevitable companion. Preserving
emotional balance calls for an ability to maintain perspective even when

events seem to progress ever more rapidly. It is also crucial for a leader to project calm and control even as the change tasks become more complex, problems accumulate, or conflict intensifies.

In periods of high-intensity change, leaders often experience extremes of emotion in rapid succession. Accumulated stress, exhaustion, and emotional turmoil can leave the leader feeling ragged and distracted, a state of mind that is apt to be a breeding ground for poor judgment. Typical signs that one is approaching the ragged edge are losing one's temper, sleep problems, and forgetting commitments, often accompanied by impulsiveness, moodiness, and indecisiveness. Signs of more serious trouble include gradual increases in consumption of alcohol, sleeping pills, or tranquilizers. A leader who is feeling ragged may make impulsive decisions that he regrets later ("I'm sorry—I just wasn't myself that day") or overlook something that he shouldn't have missed ("What was I thinking of? I can't believe I didn't stop to think about that"). At the other end of the emotional scale, the leader feels rested, focused, balanced, clear-eyed, and equipped to handle stress. His antennae are finely tuned, and he has the presence of mind to distinguish crucial information and to pursue promising diagnostic leads. His judgment is sound. Instead of feeling on the edge of a precipice, he feels securely planted on solid ground.

Knowing how to stay on a stable footing is what distinguishes leaders who flourish in times of change from otherwise good leaders who perform less well under intense pressure. These personal needs are important: a change agenda requires a leader to manage himself just as attentively as he manages his organization. A case in point is John, a high achiever at a *Fortune* 50 corporation known for its fast-moving, aggressive, and very competent management talent. John had broken every performance record in every job he held as he moved up the managerial ranks. When he reached the senior level of top one hundred managers before he was forty years old, the HR executives began betting that John would be COO within five or six years and CEO by the time he was fifty.

In most of John's previous jobs he had not been managed tightly. His bosses had recognized his talent and allowed him the freedom to be creative. In the course of a talent-planning review, the head of human resources argued that his next developmental step should be in a division outside the core business, one in a location far from corporate headquarters, as the number two to a division manager known to be tough on subordinates. The CEO thought the environment unsuited to John's abilities, and was sure that there would be tension with the division manager, but the HR head convinced him to approve the move.

John started his new job on a sour note. In their first meeting his new boss, Al, laid out his managerial rules. Al would expect a weekly memo, for his eyes only, on events of the previous week and plans for the next one. Any contact from corporate headquarters was to be reported to Al immediately, and no contact was to be initiated without Al's approval and input. John explained his close relationship with senior corporate officers, especially the chairman. Al said that what John had done before joining his division didn't matter; Al's rules prevailed now. John began to worry that he would be cut off from relationships that were very important to him. "I feel like I'm in a Boy Scout camp here," he said. "This guy treats people like children."

Over the next several months, John became more and more distressed. He chafed at Al's management style and the taboo on maintaining his relationships at corporate. Gamely, he tried to make the best of the situation by working even harder than usual. John had always been able to manage on little sleep, usually no more than four hours a night, but now he rarely slept more than two or three hours. On a trip to corporate headquarters to present his division's annual plan, John dropped in on the CEO. He said nothing negative about his new division; he put the best spin on his new assignment by restricting his comments to how much he was learning.

A month later, during John's performance review, Al listed John's accomplishments in a dry, disengaged tone. John, who prided himself on his skills as a manager and motivator, thought how much he could teach Al about motivating people. Then Al revealed John's bonus. At first John thought he had misheard the amount. He asked how Al had come up with such a low figure given the accomplishments Al had acknowledged. Al replied that John had violated one of the two rules he required his people to follow: John had visited the CEO and talked with both the CFO and head of HR. "That's disloyal and it's unacceptable," Al said.

John was stunned. He was also embarrassed to tell his wife about what had happened and the paltriness of his bonus. He thought of calling the CEO but decided that doing so would make things worse. Cut off from his support network, John felt trapped with a boss he did not respect. His characteristically high energy level dropped off, and he became increasingly withdrawn. Soon his behavior became erratic and unpredictable; he appeared to be using alcohol as a way to manage early-stage symptoms of depression.

John's story is that of a highly talented young executive who had trouble managing himself in a pressured situation he could not control. His contentious relationship with a boss whose style he resented, combined with his own ambition and self-image needs, caused John to act in a way that stopped his promising career in its tracks. A case can be made that he was put in a situation where he would be unlikely to succeed, and that the human-resources department was at fault. But in the final analysis, at this organizational level, the responsibility for figuring out how to succeed always rests with the individual in question. John did not master his political situation by figuring out how to build a winning relationship with his new boss. And he did not manage his personal needs by figuring out how to stay on an even keel even in a difficult situation that made him unhappy.

John was put in a very difficult situation that was particularly inappropriate to his personality and strengths. Could this tragedy have turned out differently? How could advice have helped? For one thing, John could have done more between learning about his new assignment and reporting. He knew little about Al and could have gathered more information about his style. In this company, managers at John's level rotate from one division to another regularly, and the chances were good that John knew someone who could have offered a preview of life in that division. He could also have sought out colleagues who reported to Al, especially other high-potential managers who expected to rotate out to another assignment eventually. But John did neither. My guess is that he believed he could handle any problem on his own. The human-resources department should also have kept an eye on the situation; at the very least, the division's HR head should have done so. They pushed John into the deep end of the pool without knowing how good a swimmer he was, and then they walked away. They should have offered help on their own, but they would have gotten more involved had John reached out to the right HR people for advice.

This chapter has laid out some fundamental principles for thinking about and managing advice. The next step is to survey the types of advice available and the kinds of advisers who can best meet the leader's needs.

CHAPTER 4

Types of Advice:
Strategic, Operational,
Political, and Personal

BARRY, THE SOFTWARE-DEVELOPMENT EXECUTIVE we met in chapter 2, used the help of advisers in areas he already knew a lot about but did not search out the expertise he needed most. Barry admitted choosing his advisers "because I could talk to them. They spoke my language." Barry sacrificed input on managing the culture, in other words, for comfort with his advisers. His mistake is common among leaders who are undiscriminating about choosing the right help to solve their most vexing challenges. Things might have turned out differently if Barry had understood his needs more accurately and matched them with care to the types of advice available. Whether new to a top job or seeking to extend a run of profitable growth, leaders' needs and problems tend to fall into the four categories outlined earlier: strategic, operational, political, and personal. Given the complexity of leaders' challenges, it is almost always a mistake to rely exclusively on one type of advice.

Strategic Advice

Corporate, not-for-profit, and government leaders frequently turn to outside consultants for help on strategy questions, such as alternatives to the organization's current path, prevailing trends and threats, and ambitious initiatives to increase competitiveness, such as acquisitions or divestitures of product lines. Good advisers are indispensable for a leader looking for just the right strategy in a high-stakes, bet-the-company situation. They can offer strategy models, research on the ramifications of alternative options, and knowledge of organizations that have pursued similar paths.

Capabilities of External and
Internal Strategic Advisers

External advisers are usually better equipped to critique the coherence and internal logic of the existing strategy than employees, who have a stake in the logic of the existing strategy. External advisers also tend to be better at distinguishing between the two strategies that always exist side-by-side: the formally articulated strategy approved by the board and the unstated de facto strategy, which exerts a more powerful influence on actual behavior and decisions. Before an outside strategic adviser arrives, the leader should prepare an explanation of the current situation, the questions that have to be answered, the stakes involved, and—to ensure better implementation and acceptance—the capabilities and attitudes of employees regarding the future path of the organization.

When external strategic advisers' capabilities fall short of expectations, it is usually because they failed to get to know the organization thoroughly enough. Outside advisers sometimes neglect to look closely at (1) how difficult it may be to implement the strategy given the organization's capabilities and resources, and (2) the culture, prevailing values, and norms that determine how things are done. This pitfall can be avoided when employees supplement the work of consultants—that is, when the leader utilizes selected managers and subordinates as internal advisers. Internal advisers can see to it that a strategy is practical (that it can succeed given the culture and limitations of the organization), that it has been formulated with an eye to its effects on employees' day-to-day challenges (which they often understand better than the leader), and that steps are in place to promote acceptance of the strategy by those who will implement it.

Employees can help a leader new to his post by describing how the current strategy was formulated, the degree that powerful managers were committed to it, and who in the company contributed. When the new leader tracks down employees who participated in formulation of the current strategy, different roles come to light, each offering a unique perspective on the strategy he has inherited. "Set-up people" paved the way for the strategy to be formulated. "Explorers" ventured into new areas to search out ideas. "Clean-up hitters" consolidated disparate ideas to create a coherent strategy or to lend it greater rigor. "Authors" formulated the strategy and may have kept records on that process. And "facilitators" helped bring the strategy to life. Finding the people who performed these functions can help the leader in two ways: by shedding light on how big ideas have previously been shaped in this particular culture and by identifying potential internal advisers.

Clarifying the Leader's Vision

Strategic advisers can also add value by helping the leader envision clearly the characteristics that the organization—and in particular its culture—ought to embody to deliver what must be achieved. This is where the leader's vision comes in. My definition of this term differs from its popular meaning. As chapter 3 suggested, a *vision* has become synonymous with a *mission* (an aspirational outcome that it is employees' duty to carry out) and an overarching *objective* (a challenging target necessary to realize the mission and supported by specific measurable goals). Both are important, but neither is a vision.

A vision is a mental image of the organization as it must become if the aspirational mission and objectives are to be achieved. It should depict vividly and memorably how people will behave, and their mind-set as they do their work and interact day to day in the ideal organization. A vision depicts what the culture should be; it is not a restatement of the long-range plan or of what will be achieved through the culture. The vision should make clear the kinds of people who will populate the organization, how its core decision-making processes will work, and how people will behave when things go well or poorly. A vision should be fleshed out enough to depict how the organization will operate at its best; to put it another way, it should resemble the screenplay for a motion picture, not the newspaper advertisement for the movie.

To arrive at this active, as-realistic-as-possible state, it should go through two rounds of clarification. First, the leader must imagine it well enough to inform his own decision making as he guides the organization forward. The clearer this vision is in the leader's mind, the more likely it is that he will recognize the types of people he needs to hire, and those he needs to let go. In the second round of clarification, the leader describes his mental image in conversations with people who test it, ask questions he hasn't thought of, and identify the forces they see in the organization that will help make it a reality or act to hinder it from seeing the light of day. The wise leader will be open to input and will encourage others to help shape the vision. He will also encourage people to form their own images based on his, in effect adding new scenes to the screenplay. With conversations and forums, the leader's original mental image will evolve into a vision that enjoys widespread understanding and common ownership.

Six months after he took the helm at IBM, Lou Gerstner famously said that the last thing the company needed was a new vision. He was referring to the typical vision statement—a general statement of intent that has little to do with the actual changes the organization needs to make. In that early period, Gerstner needed more than an aspirational slogan. He came to the job with a rough mental image of the sort of place he wanted to create and what he did not want. In order to achieve more clarity, he used his first months to talk to as many IBM people as he could. In the process, he identified those he wanted around him, sometimes elevating them several organizational levels, and those who were unlikely to be able to help. Gerstner hired people who would be loyal to him into powerful corporate staff positions and sent a signal to the organization when he fired a powerful senior manager who resisted his plan. Then he created a new top team and set out to recast the board of directors. Within his first year as CEO, he also created a special advisory group of IBM executives drawn from various parts of the corporation, a group that became his brain trust and made up for his lack of knowledge of the company and the industry. These are not moves that one makes haphazardly or randomly. Gerstner had a vision, but it was neither a mission statement nor a set of objectives. It was an image of the kind of place he wanted IBM to become, and of the types of people who could help get it there, that became clearer with each decision, success, and mistake.[1]

Using Internal and External Strategic Capabilities

The most beneficial strategic advice for a leader with a change-oriented agenda will come from three sources: (1) outside strategy consultants who bring discipline, research, and knowledge; (2) people inside the organization who offer experience and perspective; and (3) advisers, either internal or external, who help clarify the leader's vision of a culture equipped to realize the organization's mission and achieve its objectives. One *Fortune* 50 corporation's leader crafted a strategy that combined all three elements in one project.

In response to new customer needs, some companies in the industry were acquiring competitors or suppliers. Others made big investments in new products to produce enough revenue to hold their market positions. Still others formed partnerships or created new distribution organizations. This particular company, the market leader, decided to wait before taking action because its leaders were uncertain which forces would ultimately prove most influential. But in light of other companies' decisive moves, analysts, employees, and even some board members worried that being too conservative would put the company at a competitive disadvantage. The vice chairman and the most strategic of the senior managers, Chris, decided to take a closer look at the company's conservative stance. Though he had agreed that moving too quickly was unwise, he believed that the decision had been made without adequate investigation of alternative paths. Chris had used outside strategy experts to great advantage throughout his career, but this time he wanted to avoid an expensive high-visibility project in which outsiders would interview managers on an issue about which the CEO had taken a public stand.

Chris spoke to two outside advisers, both of whom he had used before but who did not know each other. He first met with each adviser separately. He explained in general terms that he had been watching what competitors were doing and wondering what those moves meant for his company. He had not yet decided what actions to take, if any. His purpose was to talk to two trusted sounding-board advisers whose different reactions would, he hoped, broaden his own thinking.

After these meetings, he decided to bring the two advisers together. One was a strategy expert who knew the industry well and had worked with its largest companies on future trends and threats. The other was an organization expert who understood the company's politics and key relationships, having helped most of its senior executives at one time or another on organization structure, culture, and their own career paths. At this joint meeting Chris took both into his confidence, explaining more clearly his ambivalence about the company's wait-and-see position, what he wanted to achieve (a thorough look at alternative paths) and what he wanted to avoid (questioning the public stance of the chairman and CEO and a political battle with his peers). He asked both advisers to come back to him with suggestions.

The advisers recommended that Chris sponsor a project in which a small group of selected employees from the part of the corporation he controlled would investigate competitors' moves, identify companies in other industries that had faced a similar situation, and lay out alternative ways to proceed. He was intrigued by the idea of using employees, since such a project could be kept confidential, under Chris's control, and insulated from the influence of other powerful senior managers until Chris became convinced of the best path forward. As the three discussed the idea, the keys to its success became clear: (1) participants who were analytical, creative, and willing to question an existing path, but loyal to the company; (2) a full-time commitment, requiring a temporary leave from their jobs, because time was short if another path was to be pursued and because the sensitivity of the strategic questions required a secrecy that was only feasible if the group was sequestered; and (3) participants who had demonstrated data-analysis abilities and willingness to question conventional wisdom and try something unprecedented. Because the participants would be asked to do something they had never done before, the group would be provided two forms of guidance: a strategic-planning model tailored to this particular task, to analyze market intelligence, draw conclusions or hypotheses, and generate recommendations; and an organizing model to orient the participants, guide them in learning from other organizations, and ensure teamwork.

Chris gained the agreement of the CEO and the CFO, who had to provide information for analysis. A dozen people were assigned to this project full-time for ninety days. The project manager was someone who had gained the confidence of the CEO and CFO. The team rented space away from corporate headquarters and agreed not to discuss their work with anyone not involved in the project, including their bosses. Models were created or adapted to analyze competitors' strategies. Outside consultants were brought in to discuss how others had approached such strategic questions, and fact-finding visits were made to companies in other industries. The outside strategy adviser provided an analytical framework, challenged the team's tentative conclusions, and guided its market analysis and financial projections. The organizational adviser provided guidance on the team's structure and processes, and on how to sell its recommendations to the senior team.

The team's final report endorsed the decision to refrain from bold moves but recommended more aggressive pursuit of certain alliances and rapid development of capabilities that could more quickly meet new market demands. Because they were formulated by employees, these recommendations exhibited a degree of practicality and cultural fit that most outsiders would have been hard-pressed to match. Of particular interest to Chris were the group's findings about competitors' strategies and how they had been formulated. He was pleased with the ability of the participants, mostly strangers to one another, to work together ad hoc under severe time pressure. Chris reviewed the recommendations with the CEO and CFO, and then described the project to the more powerful members of the senior management team. A presentation to the senior executive committee by the employee team followed. All of the team's recommendations were adopted.

The unique conditions that prevailed at Chris's company made it possible for this approach to be successful: pressure to act quickly with limited information; a powerful senior leader willing to explore new territory in an unorthodox way; and two advisers, with different but complementary abilities, able to contribute collaboratively to a creative final

FIGURE 4-1

Four types of advice

Type of advice	What the leader gains
Strategic: a vision of the future and a path to get there • Outside strategy experts: discipline, research, and external benchmarks • Insiders: experience and perspective • Advice on the culture	A better understanding of the organization's competitive strengths and weaknesses A vision of what can happen in the future, both strategically and organizationally, and a clearly articulated path to achieve it
Operational: information and techniques to maximize near-term effectiveness and efficiency • A clear, practical view of day-to-day operations • Assessment of the organization's ability to meet short-term operational goals	A better understanding of the organization's operational strengths and weaknesses Information needed to maximize day-to-day efficiency Techniques to fix short-term problems
Political: ways to utilize influence and relationships to promote acceptance of a new strategy or to improve operational effectiveness • Why people behave as they do • The nature of formal and informal structures • How groups exert power and compete	A better understanding of why people act as they do, the nature of the formal and shadow organizations, and the behavior of groups as they compete and influence one another Tools and techniques to win the support of coalitions and the loyalty of individuals
Personal: the leader's personal well-being, satisfaction, and happiness • Availability, attentiveness, and caring, all crucial at times of high stress • Openness based on trust	A safe harbor and a trusted ally A guardian of reality who can be counted on to speak sincerely and frankly

product. The short-term benefit to the company was improvement of the existing decision. A mid-term benefit was that the employees who participated learned a great deal about the marketplace, and their learning stayed within the company rather than departing with outside consultants. A longer-term benefit was the accelerated development of the participants, who gained exposure to top management that they would not otherwise have had at that point in their careers, exposure that eventually led several to be promoted unusually fast.

Bright people who are not wedded to existing ways of operating, and who are willing to ask iconoclastic questions and tackle challenging strategic problems, can be found in any organization. They represent an underutilized and often unrecognized source of strategic advice. Leaders whose organizations need help with effective and efficient day-to-day operations should look to them for operational advice.

Operational Advice

Operational advisers assess the organization's capabilities to meet its short- to mid-term goals effectively. They can provide an objective appraisal of what the organization does well or poorly with the components that drive it day-to-day, such as IT systems, financial controls, and product distribution. Whereas the time horizon of the strategic adviser is long, and the end product is a plan yet to be implemented, the operational adviser deals with problems that are occurring or threatening to occur. Such a problem might be a manufacturing bottleneck that is blocking a product from being shipped. It could be the need to drive down costs to meet budget targets for the current quarter. Or it could be the lack of timely information from field offices to inform headquarters' decisions.

Finding the Pieces of the Puzzle

An advice taker facing operational needs may have to formulate the questions to be answered, and decide how progress will be measured, in technical areas in which he is not trained. Doing so requires recruiting internal as well as external advisers to help the leader bridge gaps in his knowledge and anticipate roadblocks and tangents. When dealing with such unfamiliar areas, it is sometimes best for the leader to seek out internal help first. By doing so, he will discover people within the organization who are qualified to be involved in the eventual solutions and who might otherwise be ignored by external consultants. And he can also hone the questions that should be posed to external experts. Because the leader will have to make decisions on matters he has not fully mastered, he must have confidence in his advisers' expertise, insight, and loyalty, and must believe they will be forthright. This point is underlined by the experience of one new leader.

Diane had been a consultant to the company before joining to take over the IT department. She made an impact right away, with a sweeping reorganization that elevated younger people to replace powerful long-tenured managers. What surprised some about Diane's reorganization was that as a consultant she had been associated with the old system. But far from being a supporter, she had seen its shortcomings firsthand. Though she had never publicly expressed her disagreement with the way IT was run, she had done so privately in a way that caught the CEO's attention. He sought out Diane to discuss the future direction of information technology and what other companies were doing, usually along with the chief administrative officer to whom IT reported.

When the CAO retired, the CEO approached Diane about taking over IT. He needed a change agent, he said, someone with a broad view of how the best companies managed information and internal communications. IT would report directly to him, and she would join the senior executive group to ensure that necessary changes were dealt with openly at the highest level. It was clear to Diane that after IT was upgraded, her position would no longer report to the CEO.

Over the next couple of years, she and the CEO occasionally discussed the structure of the entire administrative staff, including IT. The CEO never revealed a preference for one organizational model or another, but asked Diane for opinions and information on how other organizations handled these functions. Eventually the CEO said that Diane had accomplished all he had hoped and that he no longer wanted IT reporting directly to him; he was ready to reorganize again. Since IT's main customers inside the company were manufacturing and distribution, he had concluded, all three units should report to the same senior executive, an EVP of Operations. That part was not a surprise, but what came next was: he offered the EVP job to Diane, pointing out that these departments had to operate differently and that her change-management abilities were just what was needed. The long-time head of manufacturing had decided to retire, he added, and Diane could install her own choice in that job.

Before becoming a consultant, Diane had worked in production and inventory-control positions in distribution departments; in her consulting career, she had seen a lot of manufacturing operations. But because she was not an expert in either distribution or manufacturing, she worried about the reactions of the people she would inherit—especially when she tried to get them to change entrenched habits. The biggest problem she faced was insufficient understanding of the root causes of the problems that plagued manufacturing. The retiring VP of manufacturing had been adept at hiding what was wrong in his department; she had known him as a difficult customer for IT. His retirement was a plus, but Diane was skeptical that the managers would reveal the department's problems to her. She worried about one question in particular: why had manufacturing productivity slowly declined over time? Because of the business mix, or the way the department was managed? She knew that maintenance costs had increased gradually; did that point to a cause of the productivity problem? The plants had always maintained high quality, but the cost of poor quality (a subset of the overall cost of quality) had steadily increased over the past two years. Why?

When her appointment was announced, Diane fielded calls from several outside consultants offering various types of help. She decided against using any right away. Instead, she approached three people on whom she had come to rely for straight and honest reactions (her "pull-no-punches advisers," as she called them). One was the former chief administrative officer, now retired. Another was the CFO, whom Diane had come to know well while working on IT budgets. The third was a senior manager in IT who had worked closely with manufacturing. She asked each what he believed to be the most important issue she faced, and was gratified that all named the productivity problem. The retired CAO suggested that she depend on the people two levels below the VP of manufacturing (not the direct reports), who were closer to the root causes of problems than anyone else. He described them as very good people who had often been intimidated by the retired head of manufacturing; as a result, their ideas had not been used as much as they should have been. He named a couple of people he thought could be helpful, and recommended that she ask others for candidates.

Using Internal Expertise to Bridge Knowledge Gaps

From her three advisers, she received the names of seven people on whom she could rely for accurate information. Over the next week, she dropped in on all seven in their offices. "I didn't want to act like the new boss who wanted everybody to come to me," Diane explained. Of the seven, she asked three to meet with her again. Her conversations with all three continued throughout her first six months in her new job, often over lunch or dinner. "They were more relaxed that way," Diane said, "and I could get them to talk more. And we could go longer and there weren't interruptions." She chose the three, she explained, because her conversations with each had taught her something new about why manufacturing operated as it did or how IT was perceived that was important enough to affect the service goals she had agreed to in her new job. Also, each provided her something unique. "Each of them had experience and a perspective quite different from what the others offered," she said. "One had been in manufacturing forever and worked in purchasing with our supplier-quality teams. He was a great historian. Another one had real breadth on the inventory-control and traffic side, and understood the flow of parts and how it all worked together. Another one had been in finance before moving over to manufacturing, and had great insight about the cost structure. I didn't plan it this way, but each of them provided a piece of the puzzle that I had to understand."

Diane also maintained contact with her three pull-no-punches advisers. At first she used them separately, mainly to verify what others were telling her. Eventually she brought them together for a series of meetings as she formulated her strategy. She also used them to help her prepare for meetings with the CEO and presentations to the board of directors.

Diane eventually brought in an outside consulting firm, but only after she had learned more about the departments and zeroed in on questions with which she needed help right away. "Of course, I came from that world and I knew what to avoid," she said. "But I had never been a client at this level and I wanted to get it right. There were things we didn't know, or didn't know how to do, that were important for our success, and we needed experts in those areas. But I wanted to be careful to spend the money I had in the right way." She would not agree to proposals for long-term projects, only to shorter ones with measurable objectives. She also stressed that the consultants had to transfer knowledge and abilities to her manufacturing people in the course of their work. She chose the only consulting firm that was specific about how it would do so, and asked the most senior consultant to meet regularly with her pull-no-punches advisers and the three mid-level managers she had tapped.

Diane said that she had learned an important lesson about using help from her internal operational advisers. "They never hesitated to lay out answers and give me a straightforward way to proceed. But I found that they didn't go beyond answering my questions. They didn't offer any more than an answer to exactly what I asked," she recalled. "When I realized that, I understood how important it was that I ask the right questions. But I didn't know enough at first to know what all the right questions were, so I asked them to tell me the questions I should be asking. That got us to a whole new level. When I was consulting, none of my clients ever asked me that question, but they should have."

Diane had been chosen for her ability to manage change, not because she possessed expert knowledge or experience in the area she took over. Making a management change for this reason sometimes leads to disaster. In her case it worked, and soon the three departments in the operations area were operating more efficiently and collaboratively than ever before. The primary explanation went beyond Diane's ability to motivate or manage her people; it also had to do with her ability to find and use the right help at the right time.

A strategic adviser can help generate a vision of what can happen in the future and a path to get there. An operational adviser can provide techniques to solve immediate problems. Both are important, but at times of fundamental change, lasting success requires more. The leader must also be adept at building coalitions, recognizing early signs of resistance, knowing who supports him (and who in turn supports them) and who doesn't and why, and understanding how his managers' needs for control affect the success of his agenda. These are not abilities that are honed by most aspiring senior leaders on the way to the top.[2] Such individuals move up on the strength of their strategic and operational abilities. Especially when one's organization must change, an additional kind of advice is called for: political advice.

Political Advice

Political advisers understand the patterns of influence that need to be harnessed to realize a new strategy or to improve operational effectiveness. Such advisers can point out the relationships that matter most to a new leader's success, equipping him to better understand how decisions are actually made, who has influence over what, and the underlying motives of managers whose support he needs. A political adviser may also compare the leader's decision-making and learning styles with the information and support system he has inherited, and suggest adaptations to make a better match, including possible staff changes. A political adviser to a veteran leader planning an ambitious change initiative might suggest a new management structure, help the leader think through how best to fill key spots, and recommend ways to prepare the organization for the required changes.

For leaders in either situation, a political adviser is also the person to turn to about the kind of culture necessary to realize the strategy, or to anticipate organizational or people-related changes needed to sustain progress. In some circumstances, it makes sense for a political adviser to collaborate with strategy and operational advisers, as happened in Chris's case. The political adviser can diagnose the interests of coalitions or cohorts whose support will be necessary, and take a reading on resistance to change. An able political adviser will usually find out more than the leader himself can about actual levels of support and managers' real degree of commitment to what the leader is advocating.

Trusted political advisers are also the people the leader turns to when the strategies he wants the organization to pursue intersect with his own career path. The political adviser can help him calculate the impact on his career of success or failure of the strategic initiatives he has undertaken. Sometimes these career inflection points present themselves as a complicated problem between a CEO and his board.

Mixed Messages and Stalled Decisions

Jeremy was a founder of the company and had been its only CEO. During his years at the helm, a string of new products had brought in impressive revenue, but expenses had grown at an even faster rate. This problem was ignored until after the IPO, when results became more transparent and investors complained about profit shortfalls. Larger corporations with more resources and greater operational discipline entered the market with less expensive products, causing sales at Jeremy's company to flatten. But because expense control had never been emphasized, costs continued to rise. It took four years of painful rationalizing and reorganizations for the company to operate more efficiently. Eventually profits began to grow again.

But all the change came at a personal cost for Jeremy. The other two founders decided to leave. The three had worked closely since designing the first prototype years earlier, and Jeremy had come to depend on their thinking, support, and friendship. They had handled most big strategic or policy matters as a group, often without the aid of ambitious formal planning projects. Everyone in the company viewed them as extensions of one another, and it was difficult to imagine it not being run by all three.

The company continued to mature, gradually adopting new processes and systems to support growth. Everything was going quite well, but Jeremy was less and less satisfied at work; he was worn out. He told his board that he wanted to step aside and asked them to come up with a plan. The board decided on an outside search to find a CEO to replace him. Six months later there was still no replacement. In the meantime, Jeremy regained his energy and told the chairman that he was enjoying his job again. The chairman wasn't certain whether that meant that the search should be suspended, but they never discussed it. Eventually two strong external candidates emerged, but one took a job elsewhere and the other was promoted when his boss learned he had received an outside offer. There were no other viable candidates in the pipeline. Jeremy believed that the board had not been aggressive enough and had lost the two best candidates because it hadn't sold them effectively. He considered his company an attractive destination and blamed a poorly managed search process. He did not express his frustration, though, and Jeremy and the chairman never discussed whether he still wanted to leave.

Several months later the company released a new product to wide acclaim. Sales and the stock price both picked up. Soon after, the highly regarded manager of engineering left for a competitor. He had hoped to be Jeremy's backup, but when he learned that the board had conducted a search instead of looking at inside candidates, he concluded that he had little chance of being promoted. Jeremy decided that the engineering department would report directly to him until a replacement was found. He also worried that the long-time EVP of sales and marketing was not equal to the challenges of an organization whose size and complexity had mushroomed. But Jeremy had never been good at delivering negative feedback, especially to loyal employees. Instead of confronting the performance problem directly, he decided to get involved in sales himself, and began spending more time in the field with salesmen.

Jeremy also had trouble sorting through the issues that landed on his desk. Decisions tended to go unmade. His managers even joked that decisions weren't made, they evolved. When Jeremy complained to his secretary that he spent more time at his desk than with customers, she pointed out that he treated all problems as equal in importance and spent too much time on matters that his subordinates should deal with. Jeremy accepted her criticism but did not know how to change. Within a year he had gone from being on the verge of stepping aside to having more direct reports, traveling more, and working longer hours.

The workload and accompanying stress caused nagging health problems, from sciatica to a persistent respiratory infection. Jeremy was uncharacteristically withdrawn at home and short-tempered at work. Again, he told the board he wanted to retire. When the chairman said that a new search so soon after the last one would not yield different results, Jeremy let out his pent-up frustration and accused the chairman of not trying hard enough. A heated exchange followed; the chairman accused Jeremy of inconsistency to the point that the board wasn't sure whether he wanted to stay or to leave. The meeting ended tensely, with no resolution.

The lead director, whom Jeremy admired, contacted him. Jeremy said he had hoped that by the time he was ready to retire, the company would be operating more smoothly than it was. He admitted that the lack of a process orientation kept decision making slow and inefficient. "I've spent years trying to stay away from big corporate life with its systems and formality. I realize now that, without some of that, we just can't get things done at our size," Jeremy said. "But I haven't laid the foundation for it or hired enough people who think that way." He had gotten angry at the chairman, he said, but was really angry at himself. The lead director replied that there hadn't been enough communication between Jeremy and the chairman, and that both sides deserved some of the blame. But the situation had reached the point that, for the good of the company and for Jeremy's own well-being, something had to be done. He recommended bringing in someone from the outside who could be objective, listen to both the board and Jeremy, and recommend how, as he put it, "you and the board can get on the same page." Jeremy agreed. The director offered to try to find someone.

Clarifying the Leader's Style, Goals, and Relationships

Jeremy had had little experience with outside help on matters like this, and did not know what to expect. He met a consultant recommended by the lead director, who had also met the chairman. When the adviser asked Jeremy who he believed should be the primary client, Jeremy or the board, Jeremy asked the adviser what he thought. The adviser said he believed it should be Jeremy, because he had the most to gain or lose and because the company, not the board, would pay for the adviser's work. Jeremy liked the sound of that, but worried how the chairman would react. The adviser said that he had posed the same question to the chairman and lead director, and had expressed the same opinion, which the directors had agreed with. Jeremy was surprised that the adviser had raised such a question directly, and recognized that he would not have risked disagreement by doing so; he would have left the situation cloudy but found a way to quietly end up in control. His approach, he realized, would have taken more time and effort. He concluded that he might benefit from working with this adviser and agreed to go ahead.

The adviser met with Jeremy and several of his direct reports to understand the company's strategy, what had to change to achieve it, and the impact on strategy of how Jeremy made decisions and managed relationships. He also spoke to each director about communication between Jeremy and the board. After a few weeks of data gathering, he and Jeremy met for their first review. "The biggest thing I got from it," Jeremy said, "was hearing problems I'd had with the board traced back to their causes." He also learned what he had done to cause the chairman to act as he had, and he came to understand their interchanges better from the chairman's point of view. The adviser, he added, "kept going back to how I could have done things differently and avoided all this angst."

The adviser sat in on top team and board meetings, accompanied Jeremy to field offices, and spoke again with senior managers and directors. Then he and Jeremy met again, this time to deal more directly with Jeremy's style and his relationship with the board. The adviser began by asking rhetorically why Jeremy had been indecisive and frustrated during the succession process but clear, adept, and decisive on the field visit and in senior-management meetings. In the latter situations, the adviser noted,

Jeremy had managed the conversation in such a way that he gradually clarified the path he wanted to take.

The adviser speculated that Jeremy's decision-making pattern was to approach clarity on important matters in stages: first he'd lock onto a general hypothesis; then he'd test it and move to a firm position; next he would engage in a give-and-take conversation in which he would pose a question, someone would respond, Jeremy would build on the answer and ask another question, others would give him more input, and so forth. Eventually he would piece together a mosaic and settle on a path. His past success was probably due to routine use of this kind of pattern with the other founding partners. But on the question of his succession, he had never reached clarity on the initial hypothesis, nor had he initiated give-and-take dialogue with the board. As a result, Jeremy had not reached closure on his future role in the company, which was necessary for the board to be able to move forward.

The adviser added that the chairman and lead director believed the board could not pursue a succession plan until it heard from Jeremy whether he wanted to stay at the company in some capacity or leave. For that to happen, the adviser said, a way had to be found to initiate the kind of give-and-take that could help Jeremy decide on his preference. The board seemed willing to do whatever Jeremy wanted, he continued, but it did not know what that might be and was not doing a good job of asking. Jeremy admitted that he was unsure himself.

In subsequent meetings, Jeremy and the adviser discussed his plans for the future and the legacy he hoped to leave at the company. Discussing these topics with someone who was neither a subordinate nor a director freed Jeremy to explore them in new ways. He read articles and books the adviser brought him about how other leaders had handled what Jeremy was going through. He also met with two retired CEOs to discuss their transitions. Jeremy gradually realized that he did not want to leave until the company reached its next level of growth and operating effectiveness, and he articulated the benchmarks that would signify that goal. He also admitted that he alone could not lead the company to those levels, and that he needed someone beside him with abilities different from his own.

Jeremy believed he had found the basis for an answer to the succession question, but he was worried that the chairman would resist it. The adviser replied that they had only accomplished half of their task; the other half was to figure out how to approach the directors to guarantee an end result that they and Jeremy would be happy with. For that to happen, Jeremy had to describe clearly what he wanted, as well as his fears and reservations, and to listen to the chairman's point of view.

Jeremy suggested that the adviser talk with the chairman alone. The adviser refused; what was most important, he said, was the give-and-take between Jeremy and the chairman. He would attend the meeting if Jeremy and the chairman wanted him there, but Jeremy must take responsibility. "It's the only way for you to get what you want in this situation. If you don't get out on point to deal with this," the adviser said, "you can't blame anyone but yourself if things don't work out." They agreed that Jeremy and the adviser would meet with the lead director. After preparation of a draft white paper summarizing their discussion, the lead director and Jeremy would meet with the chairman. If they agreed, a final white paper signed by both Jeremy and the chairman would be sent to the board.

At its next meeting, the board agreed on a succession plan. Its decision was to find an executive vice president to lead sales, marketing, R&D, and business development—all the areas on which future growth depended. If the new EVP performed well, he or she would become chief operating officer, with the four business units as direct reports, a year later. A year after that, Jeremy would hand over the CEO title but remain on the board.

At this writing, the new EVP is eight months into his first year. He and Jeremy have worked together well, and he has begun to build solid relationships inside the organization. He came from a company of the size that Jeremy's hopes to reach; to Jeremy's relief, the new EVP, though accustomed to the discipline and systems necessary at that size, is pleased to be at a less formal organization and committed to keeping it from becoming bureaucratic. He appears to be on a sure path to be named COO.

What happened here? Jeremy was stymied because he had not built a relationship with the chairman that would enable him to address a potentially contentious problem, important to the company and emotionally trying for himself. And he had not created a forum that would enable him, given his style, to define clear preferences. Jeremy didn't initiate a search for help—the lead director convinced him of the need for an adviser—but he went along. Although it was an ingrained feature of his style to avoid disagreement (he tried twice to convince the adviser to talk to the chairman on his behalf), he accepted feedback on this point and then handled the issue himself with the adviser helping by providing a plan and some counsel. Unlike Diane's situation, resolution did not depend on asking the right questions or applying better methods. It was a matter of understanding his political situation and of crafting a solution that met others' needs as well as his own and matched his decision-making style. Doing so required factoring in the relationships, emotions, and needs for control of the people involved; understanding how the chairman saw things; grasping the impact of his own emotions; being open to feedback and willing to be influenced; and having a plan to gain agreement.

The fourth type of advice deals directly and exclusively with the leader's emotions and underlying motivations.

Personal Advice

A leader's source of personal advice is often a spouse, relative, or close friend who simply cares about his well-being. Within the intimate confines of a long-standing trusting relationship, the leader can let her guard down and reveal emotions and conflicts that ordinarily remain under wraps. The personal adviser's insight and support may prompt the leader to share even more. The result can eventually be a deep bond of trust, and sometimes the relationship comes to play an important role in how the leader leads the organization. An example is the relationship between Bess Truman and her husband Harry when he was president of the United States. Clark Clifford, a political adviser to Truman, put it this way: "Bess Truman was a pillar of strength to her husband, a person of sound judgment to whom he was devoted. Because she was so retiring in public, most people did not realize how important her role was in President Truman's life. They made a splendid team. President Truman was not always analytical or sufficiently detached in evaluating the people around him. Mrs. Truman often had better insight than her husband into the quality and trustworthiness of the people who were gathered around him, and helped to steer him away from the people [who might have gotten the Administration in trouble]."[3]

Coping with High Expectations

Personal advice is particularly important for a new leader, especially one hired from the outside. Expectations are high: subordinates form early impressions of the new leader before they get to know him, and his boss expects quick successes to verify that his hiring decision was sound. The leader may also have inherited an administrative support and information system unsuited to his learning or decision-making style. Along with the normal anxieties of forming new relationships, the result can be a high level of stress. At such times, having a reliable source of personal advice can make all the difference. But it is all too common for leaders in high-stress situations not to have such a relationship in place in advance and then to overlook a willing prospective personal adviser, as Dave did in chapter 2.

Is a personal relationship between a leader and adviser important? Will the adviser be at his best if he doesn't like or respect the leader? To what degree does friendship matter? It depends on the type of help. For strategic and operational needs, the questions tend to point to clear choices ("All things considered, is it best for us to go in this direction or that one?" or "what do we need to know that we don't today about how to get our costs down?"), and advisers' input typically consists of knowledge or opinions. In these cases, the relationship between the leader and his adviser is less important.

It can matter a lot, though, when the leader is facing political challenges, particularly when they are important enough to him personally to engage his emotions. If, for example, he is competing with peers for a promotion, or resistance to the changes he wants to make has caused influential coalitions to line up against him, he must trust his adviser enough to share worries and feelings he would normally conceal. If he has to change his behavior to deal with such threats, he may look to his political adviser to guide his efforts. The more changes he must make, or the harder it is for him to act differently, the more the adviser will have to prod him, testing the relationship. The stronger the bond between them, the more likely they will be able to see it through.

It is even more likely that personal needs will require a close relationship between leader and adviser. The story of Wayne in chapter 2 described how a leader's emotions can affect his judgment at the most critically important times. Without a safe harbor, needed perspective can be elusive. At these times in particular, the adviser may be the only person who can deliver difficult feedback to the leader or reveal what others see but the leader is blind to. At such times, the adviser assumes the role of guardian of reality. In order to point out a reality that the leader cannot see, or does not want to see, there must be an established bond with the adviser that opens up his thinking and enables him to gain a new perspective. Consider the case of Curt.

The Stresses of the Spotlight

Curt graduated from an elite university in Germany and earned a doctorate in statistics and economics. After four years at an international consulting firm in Paris, he earned a degree at INSEAD. Curt then joined a financial-services company at its European headquarters. After two years and a string of successes, he spent eighteen months at the company's U.S. headquarters. Over the next six years, he opened a new office in Australia and ran a large U.S. office. Curt was then chosen to join the newly created office of the chairman, which encompassed the chairman/CEO, the vice chairman/CFO, and an executive vice president who ran several lines of the business. The CEO was sixty-two, the CFO fifty-nine, and the EVP fifty-three; Curt was forty-six.

His appointment was a surprise to those who had expected someone more senior in age and with more tenure to be selected. Curt had been with the company for a dozen years and had held five different jobs. It was widely assumed that the EVP/business-unit head was being groomed as the next CEO—company policy mandated a retirement age of sixty-five for a CEO—and that the CFO would stay on for a few years in his current job and then retire too. Curt's promotion prompted speculation that he was in line to become the next number two. Many experienced senior managers were anxious to take the measure of this young European.

Curt was as confident as he was bright. He spoke four languages fluently and could hold his own with anyone intellectually. His record at the company was unblemished. The only less-than-positive comment in his 360-degree feedback was that he could be aloof and not reveal his thoughts and feelings. Curt's first six months in his new job were fast-paced; he had much to learn and significant responsibilities to take hold of. He worked hard to master his new assignment and, characteristically, seemed to do so effortlessly. It was not apparent to others how stressed he felt or how many hours he was putting in.

Curt prided himself on resourcefulness and independence, but the pressure of his new job and his lack of leisure or a social outlet was starting to affect him. He sensed that his judgment was less surefooted, and he was uncharacteristically indecisive. Since his 360-degree evaluation, Curt had worked hard to become more self-aware and develop his interpersonal skills. Evaluating himself now, he worried that stress and the corporate spotlight would cause him to make a blunder that his political competitors could take advantage of. He decided to extend a trip to Europe to visit his mother in Germany.

Finding an Outlet: Speaking Freely and Listening Actively

Curt's mother had been the anchor of his family. She had devoted herself to providing for her sons' educations after their father's death, and had always been available to help them or simply to talk. Curt's original reason for visiting his hometown had been simply to relax. But during their first evening together, in the flat where he had lived as a child, he told her about his life in America and became uncharacteristically emotional. "Something like that had never happened to me before. I began talking to my mother, in this place where I had felt so secure, with the same furnishings, even the same smells from her cooking," he later recalled. "I admitted to her that I was proud of what I had accomplished but that I was also very lonely, that I could trust no one and had no outlet, no way to be with anyone who I could just unload to about what I was going through." They talked until early morning and most of the next day. Curt described his fear of failure, the tension of avoiding any sign of weakness, and his worry about the toll on his judgment. Curt's mother listened carefully and prompted him to talk further by asking questions.

Eventually his mother offered an opinion. She said that Curt's high expectations of himself even as a child had caused her to worry about him. She went on, he recalled later, to point out "that I was the person who was putting pressure on myself, not the political competitors at work. By doing that, she said, I was playing into their hands. She said that the way things sounded to her, they really didn't have to do anything to get me to fail, that I would do that all by myself. But even if I didn't mess up, the toll it was taking on me was going to hurt me in the long run, that I couldn't go on having no life outside of work and just putting more and more pressure on myself. These were things that I had thought of, but when my mother said them, they had more impact than anything I could ever have thought myself."

Curt flew back to the United States feeling better than he had in some time. The few days with his mother had given him new perspective. He had noticed too how relaxed he had been listening to her counsel, probably because she was the first unequivocally trustworthy person he had spoken to in some time. Over the next few months, Curt tried to find more time for social relationships. He was only partially successful because his work habits were deeply ingrained, but he made progress. Curt had been invited by the company to a fundraising reception at the city's largest hospital. Talking with the doctors and trustees, he decided to become involved, eventually serving on several committees. His dedication, hard work, and financial contributions earned him an invitation to become a trustee. Given his travel schedule and responsibilities, he had little time for other activities, but the hospital was enough.

The CEO is a year from retirement, and Curt seems likely to take on more responsibility. If he does, there will be many explanations for his success. One of them will be his visit to his mother. Her active listening and attention to his emotional needs encouraged Curt to reveal what was on his mind, and her counsel had an impact on him that no one else could have matched. And Curt deserves credit too. He recognized that he needed a change and reached out to his mother. Then he listened to her without defensiveness or rationalization.

This chapter has surveyed the first component of a comprehensive framework for advice taking: four types of advice that match the four needs of a leader with a change mission—strategic, operational, political, and personal. It has also offered portraits of how different leaders managed the advice they solicited. Now we will turn to the second part of the framework: the kinds of people who offer advice.

CHAPTER 5

Kinds of Advisers:
Expert, Experienced,
Sounding-Board, and Partner

DIFFERENT KINDS OF ADVISERS assume different roles in a helping relationship, and each role calls for the leader to interact with the adviser in a particular way. In each case, the leader's success at managing the relationship will go a long way toward determining whether or not he receives useful, actionable help. And the first step in managing helping relationships adeptly is to figure out what kind of adviser one needs to deal with a particular kind of problem.

The Expert Adviser

Some advisers are set apart by their expertise. They have studied a given area—it could be quality control or budgeting or the organization culture—in depth and detail, and they understand its variations and grasp how its components interrelate. The best of them can explain their specialty clearly. A leader looking for an expert adviser should have prepared a set of questions to compare his needs with the scope and depth of the adviser's expertise. Diane, whom we met in chapter 4, used this technique skillfully when she met with seven potential in-house operational advisers and settled on the three whose specialized knowledge and helpful attitudes would best help her to solve her operational puzzle.

To extend the health-care analogy we used in chapter 4, the leader resembles a patient with undiagnosed symptoms. The first step is to see a primary-care physician. If the primary-care level of expertise is enough, the process may end there. But if the patient's symptoms exceed the scope of primary care, the patient will consult a specialist with more experience diagnosing the disorders that his symptoms point to. This does not mean that the specialist is necessarily a better physician; it only means that she has more appropriate expertise. If the specialist orders tests, she may consult other specialists or researchers with even more fine-gauged knowledge about the results. In the final analysis, the well-being of the patient depends on the match between the diagnostic question and the expertise of each doctor on the team. Like a patient at the beginning of the diagnostic process, a leader preparing to change an organization knows he needs help, but typically has only a rough sense of the specifics. For answers, he looks to people with more expertise than he possesses. What is the best way to prepare to do so? The first step is to learn more about the areas of specialization that advisers offer.

Chapter 4 described four types of advice that correspond to basic managerial needs. What should the leader look for in an adviser in each area? Because three of the four realms—strategic, operational, and political—are founded on concrete bodies of knowledge, a general familiarity with each will help the leader to match his needs with experts' specialties.

The Strategy Expert

Strategy experts should understand the nature and evolution of the industry, the technologies on which its products or services are based, and the economics that drive it (particularly its cost structures, points at which economies of scale become important, and the impact of volume growth on profits or break-even points). They should be able to spell out in detail the long-term financial implications of one path or another. Strategy advisers to not-for-profit and governmental leaders should also have mastered the budgeting process and the intricacies of budget approval, the underlying principles on which policies are founded, the impact on strategy of various stakeholders, and technologies that can improve implementation of policy or delivery of services.

Strategy experts should also have a deep familiarity with the company's direct competitors, organizations that could become competitors, and those whose activities affect the company's fortunes. They should be aware of social trends that could have an impact on the organization. And they need sufficient systems-analysis expertise to see the leader's situation as a network of interdependent parts, and to assess the sensitivity of particular segments of the organization to problems or actions in other areas. They should also grasp the relative benefits of alternative strategies, such as whether expanding through acquisition or growing organically by investing in R&D or cutting manufacturing costs would give the company a sharper edge given current and expected market conditions.

Diagnosis of internal strengths and weaknesses, knowledge of industry trends, and analysis of competitors' vulnerabilities are indispensable skills for capable strategy experts. Truly useful strategy experts also contribute substantially to a compelling strategic mission and high-level objectives. Strategy expertise begins to add value with a well-thought-through battle plan that makes challenging aspirations appear achievable. But even those strategists who reach the value-added level are only smart strategists—not expert advisers—if they do not offer more. The best strategy advisers are also good teachers: they discern how the leader learns, and work hard at making complicated analysis understandable and paths to greater competitive strengths clearer. They shape their ideas and proposals so that the leader will recognize strategic options he did not know existed. Expert strategy advisers offer information, analysis, and opinions in such a way that the leader gains insight he may not get any other way, better equipping him to see how strategy recommendations can be made actionable.

The Operations Expert

Operations experts have mastered particular aspects of the organization's day-to-day functioning. Regardless of his specialty, an operations expert will concentrate on how things work, what it will take to operate more efficiently, and the resources used or costs expended as the product or service moves toward the customer. Whereas an expert in strategy analyzes current conditions and anticipates the direction of trends to help determine how the organization should pursue its goals, the operations expert concentrates on problems that block it from fulfilling its immediate and near-term commitments.

Experts can be found to analyze virtually every activity of the organization. A study done in the early 1970s for the American Management Association listed 101 different management-consulting specialties.[1] The growth of the consulting business and of technology over intervening decades guarantees that the number of specialties is much greater today. Take, for example, auditors, who should offer a thorough understanding of the financial structure through which all of the organization's activities can be measured and accounted for. They provide expertise in general accounting (including the general ledger, accounts receivable and payable, and general selling and administrative expenses), cost accounting (including pricing inventories, product or service cost data, and a job order cost system), long-range financial projections (for sales, expenses, and return on revenue or equity), financial reporting and control (forecasting, budgeting, or cash estimates), and capital investment (asset allocation and working capital). Good financial operational experts may specialize in one or two of these categories, but will be able to explain the impact on current operations and on the general financial health of the organization of any of them. They will also be able to identify the subcategories with the greatest relevance to the strategy the leader has chosen to pursue, and to spell out what it would take to strengthen the organization's abilities in each case. Financial operational experts can be particularly important, for example, in establishing compliance with Sarbanes-Oxley-related regulations, which demand a high level of transparency and specificity in financial reporting. Corporations turned to their outside auditors for guidance when they put new controls in place to comply with the new law.

For a leader seeking operational help, it is useful to think in terms of three grades of advisers. First are the experts whose knowledge equips them to diagnose problems, analyze conditions to clarify root causes, and prescribe a solution. Advisers at the next level can do the same and also implement the solutions they recommend; because they expect to be accountable for their recommendations, these level-two experts are more likely to be precise and practical in what they suggest. Third-level experts combine the skills of the other two with the ability to train others, thus leaving behind capabilities and knowledge.

Operations experts tend to be highly specialized. To derive the most help from them, the leader should first take pains to determine whether he needs an expert merely to point out what is called for (which is often adequate when the organization itself has people with good execution skills), to solve a tough problem (usually necessary in a crisis or when in-house problem-solving skills are insufficient), or to train managers and employees (typically a function of time available, employees' capability, and the organization's culture).

The Political Expert

Political experts draw on a body of knowledge that has three areas of focus: (1) why people behave as they do, (2) the nature of formal and in-formal organization structures, and (3) how groups of people exert power and compete.

Human Behavior.   Among the many sources of insight into human be-havior, one that is particularly relevant for the political expert and the leader with a change agenda is the work of Harvard's David McClelland and those who applied his work to the challenges of organizational change. McClel-land identified three basic needs that drive us all in varying degrees and con-figurations: the need for achievement (to win, compete, or pursue unique achievements), the need for affiliation (to be accepted or identified with a particular social group), and the need for power (to get others to do our bidding, either for the good of the whole—socialized power—or to en-hance one's own personal power). McClelland's research was fundamental to management development as we know it today. Beginning in the 1960s, his work spawned the first attempts at measuring organizational climate (as opposed to tracking employee opinions) and correlating it with managerial motivation and behavior.[2] McClelland's insight into the impulses and needs that cause people to behave as they do helped set the tone for much of the applied organization-development work of the last several decades.[3] Daniel Goleman, who studied under McClelland, has extended our understand-ing of political behavior through his work on emotional intelligence, a model of organizational and political maturity.[4] As advances in technology enable researchers to explain more about the human brain, Goleman is exploring its biology and neural chemistry to better understand how we make choices in the relationships that shape the political aspect of our organizational lives.

Organization Structures.   Understanding the nature of organizations begins with how they evolved. The foundations of today's organizational structures can be traced to a handful of early modern institutions like the Catholic Church, the traditions of European monarchies, and the military. They are the original sources of the concepts that authority increases as one moves up in an organizational structure and that there should be only one person in charge of any particular unit. Business borrowed from the military the distinction between line and staff responsibility, and from monarchies and organized religion the attribution to a leader of power to ascribe broad meaning and purpose to our activities. These organizational principles were unquestioned for centuries. Not until the 1960s did the U.S. aerospace industry recognize that in some situations better results emerged from a shared-power, two-boss structure, giving birth to the matrix organization.

Political advisers should be aware that the evolution of organization structure tells only part of the story of how an organization works, the part that traces information flows through a chain of command and the expected development path for people in the organization. But as political advisers recognize, information flow and decision-making processes are not formal and vertical but interactive, circuitous, and horizontal. Gerry Egan, a psychologist at Loyola University of Chicago, coined the term *shadow organization* to characterize the real-world relationships and communication patterns that parallel the formal structure.[5]

In considering a political adviser's organizational expertise, the leader should assess his understanding of and experience with both the formal organization structure and the shadow organization. Does he understand the variants of formal structure and the benefits of each? Does he know how each originated and the purposes for which it was designed? Is he able to walk through the organization and observe the operation of the formal structure with enough acuteness to describe its inefficiencies? Does he pick up misconnections in the work process because the structure is not aligned with the organization's purpose and primary objectives? Is he able to describe the shadow organization, including how people interact across and in spite of organizational boundaries? Is he well schooled in the various ways that the parallel structure operates in sync with the formal structure?

Power.   A political expert should be able to diagnose accurately the methods individuals and groups use to acquire, keep, or restore control and influence over others. People who wield influence well over those around them determine the direction of the organization and its ability to change and develop over time. Political experts observe how the leader exerts influence and the subtle means he uses to get others to do what he wants them to do (which the leader himself is often blind to). They may speculate about why seeking to control and influence others is important to him and what needs are satisfied by doing so. Is it primarily a need to compete, or to attain a certain status for the organization, or to be admired and accepted by people whose approval is important? Perhaps it is to gain personal benefit, the symbols of power, reputation, or position. Whatever the leader's primary needs—they are always multiple—and the clearer his advisers are about them, the more they will be in a position to help.

Understanding motives is just one dimension of using and keeping power. Others are values, habits, skills, and emotional hardiness, especially resilience. Political advisers should familiarize themselves with the particular signs that indicate the leader's shifting capabilities and needs at any given time.

It is also important for a political-expert adviser to understand how people in positions of power use counsel and the organizational mechanisms they depend on to exert influence. The use of counsel to acquire and hold power has a long, rich history, with which the political adviser should be familiar; particularly relevant is how Machiavelli, Sun Tzu, and Aristotle provided counsel to kings and warriors. Modern leaders have also used their advisers to gain influence and control; examples include Franklin Roosevelt and Louis Howe, Dwight Eisenhower and

Sherman Adams, John Kennedy and his brother Robert, and George W. Bush and Karl Rove.

The inner workings of government can shed light on the organizational mechanisms that advisers employ to help the leader gain and stay in power. One study of the policy-making mechanisms of the British prime minister's office found four decisive factors in the prime minister's ongoing ability to dominate: (1) that his policies reflected the prevailing climate of ideas in the nation, and that his advisers read that climate accurately; (2) that few destabilizing events occurred, and that if they did happen his advisers and ministers reacted well; (3) that he won the support of powerful interests, and that his advisers interpreted those interests accurately and protected the prime minister as necessary; and (4) that his advisers were able and supportive but neither conspicuous nor overwhelmingly powerful outside of the prime minister's office.[6] It is easy to discern how each point applies to leaders of corporate or not-for-profit organizations.

Much can also be learned about power from great social-change organizers like Mohandas Gandhi and Nelson Mandela, who, without armies or the economic threat of trade sanctions, changed the course of societies and toppled governments largely on the strength of the values they represented. Saul Alinsky, an astute and effective Chicago-based community and union organizer active from the 1940s through the 1960s, was particularly good at recognizing and exploiting his opponents' weaknesses, usually before they recognized their own vulnerabilities, something that can benefit anyone competing for any goal. A program Alinsky ran in the 1960s, known as "the school for radicals," trained many of the social-change organizers of the next decade.[7] (For a thought-provoking treatment of ways to master the political environment, see his *Rules for Radicals*, a modern-day update of Machiavelli's *The Prince*.)

In sum, an expert adviser has in-depth knowledge of one of three realms: strategic, operational, or political. A leader hoping to tap that knowledge begins by analyzing his situation to determine which specialty is most pertinent to his change agenda and challenges. Then, for each relevant area, he should list what he currently knows, what he assumes but is unsure of, and what he wishes to gain and to avoid by finding out more. These steps will help prepare him to select the right expert

FIGURE 5-1

Four kinds of advisers

Kind of adviser	What the leader gains
Expert: deep knowledge of strategy, operations, or political processes. Three grades of expertise: 1. Diagnose, analyze, and recommend 2. Also implement recommendations 3. Also transfer knowledge and train others	• **Strategic:** broad industry knowledge, a model for weighing strategic options, complexity made understandable • **Operational:** detailed knowledge of day-to-day organization functions, techniques to solve immediate problems, ways to operate more efficiently • **Political:** better understanding of human behavior, the nature of formal and informal structures and processes, and how groups exert power and compete
Experienced: first hand experience of the pressures the leader is experiencing and a grasp of what it takes to succeed	• Advice from a peer who understands what the leader is up against (often most beneficial to a new leader)
Sounding-board: objective and trusted counsel and feedback, dependence on the leader's description of situations he faces, safe harbor	• Objective feedback, active listening, support, recognition of the leader's emotions
Partner: close association with the leader to implement changes and to get to know the organization deeply	• Active involvement in implementation, commitment to results, tailored and practical advice, informed feedback

adviser. But gaining knowledge alone will not be sufficient to help the leader with a change agenda. Equally important are skills, behavior, and a temperament adapted to a protracted set of challenges. Sometimes talking with someone who has been in the same spot can help.

The Experienced Adviser

Advisers' credibility typically flows from what they know, but it can be even more compelling when they have been in situations similar to, or more difficult than, what the leader faces. Often those who have the most wisdom to offer have had the most experience. One example is Clark Clifford, who was called upon to advise four U.S. presidents: Franklin Roosevelt, Harry Truman, John Kennedy, and Lyndon Johnson. Truman, who as vice president had not been involved in policy setting, and

Kennedy, who had had limited experience in Washington, found it particularly helpful early in their first terms to talk with someone who had advised their predecessors. Sometimes it is even more enlightening to talk with the former leader himself; Kennedy, for example, consulted both Eisenhower and Truman during the dangerous days of the Cuban Missile Crisis.

Experts and experienced advisers interact differently with the leader, and the leader's responsibilities differ as well. With an expert adviser, it is up to the leader to specify the adviser's mission and objectives clearly, to ask the right questions, and to listen carefully. An experienced adviser, by contrast, is more like a peer, offering a firsthand perspective rather than expert knowledge. I have seen many instances in which a leader (myself included) benefited from his predecessor's advice, but benefit is assured only when the leader manages the relationship. Most predecessors want to help, but they hesitate to offer unsolicited advice to avoid appearing critical or suggesting that their own tenures were more successful. In most cases, the leader must approach the predecessor with an explicit request for information or input. Leaders who take responsibility for the relationship also draw out appropriate lessons rather than expect the predecessor to pinpoint the most pertinent analogy from his own experience. The key is "active listening"—encouraging the adviser to reflect on what he did in a similar situation.[8] Jay is an example.

A Predecessor's Insight

Jay had just taken over the largest division of a retail corporation. His predecessor had been promoted to chief operating officer and remained Jay's immediate boss. Their relationship was mutually respectful but strained; in fact, Jay believed that he had been promoted without his boss's endorsement because the CEO wanted Jay in the division president's job. The person who had recruited Jay to the company, Frank, had retired after having served as corporate COO and, before that, president of the division Jay now headed. Jay's current boss had reported to Frank in both positions. Not only had Frank held Jay's job; he had also managed Jay's boss.

Jay had stayed in touch with Frank after his retirement. This time Jay contacted him to discuss an acquisition opportunity, one that promised to be the largest and most complex deal Jay had attempted. Because Frank had managed a number of similar deals, Jay asked Frank to meet with him. Well into the conversation, Frank asked how things were going with Jay's boss. Jay's hesitation told Frank that the answer was not positive. Jay said afterward that he had paused to weigh whether to be forthcoming about the relationship with his boss. He could have deflected the question ("It's early—we'll make it work") without deceit. But because he trusted Frank and was troubled by the relationship, he decided to put his cards on the table. Jay described situations in which his boss had second-guessed Jay's decisions and "never seemed satisfied with anything I did. I've never gotten any positive feedback." Jay's conversation with Frank went something like this:

Jay: You hired him into the company?

Frank: Yes, I met him when I was recruiting at his college. I hadn't seen anyone who looked like a real winner, and he was the last one to come in. We talked for two hours and then I took him to dinner. I hired him, and he worked for me for his first five years here.

Jay: So you were impressed with him.

Frank: He grew on me. He wasn't very polished. He'd come from a poor family and struggled to get to where he was. People had always overlooked him. And that just made him work harder.

Jay: I didn't realize that about him. It sounds like you saw something you didn't see in other people you were interviewing.

Frank: Absolutely. My sense was that he'd get to where he needed to go, no matter how hard he had to work or how difficult it was. But he did it in a quiet way, never flashy.

Jay: You thought he had something special that the company needed?

Frank: He had determination and a real intense drive, but he was very quiet back then. I learned later it was because he just didn't trust anyone. He'd been rejected so much that he kept things bottled up. But I sensed that he was real competitive and knew how to work hard, and was very smart, and had very good values.

Jay: So you decided to work on this lack-of-trust part of him?

Frank: It was why he didn't reveal a lot about what he was thinking. But he knew the right answer nine times out of ten. He was used to doing everything on his own—it took him a long time to learn to get to the same objective through other people. When he figured out that the only way to move up was by managing people, he worked hard at it. It's not natural for him.

Jay: So you saw progress, or you wouldn't have kept promoting him. But it sounds like he didn't get as far as you had hoped.

Frank: Well, his personality didn't change. But he's had a pretty successful run here, and six or seven people who he managed did real well under him. [Frank named several who were now running other companies.]

Jay: I didn't realize those guys had worked under him. That's impressive.

Frank: He was pretty tough on all of his people. But there were some who figured out how to get a lot of help from him, and they're where they are today because of it.

Jay: They did something to get him to trust them?

Frank: The ones who did it best figured out that he had a lot to offer them. They asked him what he thought about things, and kept him informed so he was never surprised. They went to him with things, instead of expecting him to take the initiative, but eventually the relationship became more of a give-and-take. I'm pretty sure every one of those people who are now presidents somewhere else still stay in touch with him.

Jay summarized this conversation by saying that he had learned more about his boss in a half-hour with Frank than he had in four years of working for him. He realized that he had more to gain than his boss did, and that it was up to him to make it work. "What I finally understood," he said, "was that other people who had been in the same spot had gotten a lot more from him than I was. This thing about trust was as important as anything else. I realized I wasn't doing my part to make this work, and that I had to go more than halfway." Jay's insight came about largely because Frank had provided the right level of detail; that happened in turn because of Jay's attentive responses to each of Frank's comments. Jay had listened actively, responding in a way that indicated he was listening carefully, wanted to hear more, and wanted a deeper understanding, all of which in turn caused Frank to reveal more.

For new leaders, experienced advisers tend to be most useful early in their tenures when they are first taking hold, especially in a new organization. For those who have occupied their positions for a while and now face new challenges, experienced advisers can point to relevant pitfalls and resources with which they have firsthand experience. Though experienced advisers have much to offer, these relationships are not common; they also tend to be more sporadic than continuous, for reasons that originate with both participants. Some leaders whose predecessors have retired, for example, rarely turn to them because they want to prove they can do a better job, especially if radical change is needed. They take note of past mistakes and decisions that did not pan out, often with consequences that the new leader is left to deal with. And leaders who must undo what their predecessors put in place rarely reach out.

Finding Experienced Advice

Is it possible to find an experienced adviser who is not one's predecessor? Few new leaders have the time to search. As for experienced former leaders themselves, some are so accustomed to making decisions themselves, and to being in charge rather than in the background, that despite their management and leadership skills they are not equipped to be advice givers. Furthermore, former leaders' advice is usually limited to what succeeded or failed for them; rarely have they thought broadly about change, or witnessed a wide range of situations. But in spite of these cautions, if you can find someone who has been in your shoes, who understands firsthand what it's like, and, crucially, listens and concentrates on your success rather than reliving his own experiences, figure out a way to utilize what he has to offer.

Another source of experienced advisers is current leaders. The Young Presidents Organization was helpful to me years ago; today several national network-based organizations also serve the same purpose. Some universities also provide similar opportunities. Jeff Miller at Boston University pioneered the Manufacturing Roundtable, an industry–academic collaboration, in the early 1980s. It exposed leaders of manufacturing companies to the latest operations research and enabled them to form helpful relationships with counterparts at other companies. Less formal groups can also be fruitful. I once realized that I was advising eight people whose situations and styles were remarkably similar; another shared circumstance was that none of them had anyone but me to talk to about their big organizational problems or their careers. All of them responded enthusiastically to my offer to bring them together. As a result of our meetings, most stayed in touch with one another, and some formed sounding-board relationships that lasted for years.

The Sounding-Board Adviser

A sounding-board adviser serves the leader as a kind of high-definition mirror, reflecting back objective reactions to the situations the leader recounts and the emotions he expresses. What the leader gains is insights that are more readily apparent to an observer than to her ("You're trying to keep it under control, but you're upset about this. maybe it's anger, maybe frustration . . ."). The reactions of a sounding-board adviser can also help the leader zero in on the next step in a complex situation ("It sounds like, when you come right down to it, what you really want to happen here is . . .").

Because distance from the situation is a component of their value to the leader, sounding boards typically do not belong to the leader's organization. As noted earlier, advisers in this role are often spouses, partners, or close friends. Sometimes, though, a leader will find an employee who can fulfill this role, as I did years ago when I moved into the top spot. Jim Richard offered political advice in my advice network. He joined the company to fill two roles: first, to offer our clients his experience as a former CEO of a midsize manufacturing company and, later, as head of human resources at a major corporation; and, second, to help me change the culture of the company. Because he was an employee, attending meetings and walking the halls, he continuously took readings of the company's political climate and morale. These observations made his counsel even more valuable. Though Jim also functioned as an experienced adviser and an expert with our clients, and as a partner adviser in change efforts within the company, his biggest value to me was as a sounding board. When I needed to test out an idea that wasn't yet ready for other people to hear, or just to express frustration or worry, Jim was there. He listened well and patiently, but was empathic enough to pick up on my urgency. He didn't judge my motives, but never hesitated to give me straight feedback. Availability, skillful listening, patience, an unjudgmental stance, frank feedback, empathy—these are the characteristics that made Jim a great sounding board, and the model for that role I have used ever since.

The first prerequisite for valuable advice from a sounding-board adviser is sufficient trust for the leader to reveal all aspects of the situations he is facing and the emotions (pride, anger, irritation, frustration, even fear) that impact his decision making. The second requirement is the adviser's objectivity, which is grounded in his relative separateness from the leader's situation.

Personal advisers, who see the leader at his most reflective and revealing moments and want to be helpful, often take on the role of sounding board. If their advice is to be genuinely helpful, a third condition needs to be met: over time, the leader must share with his personal adviser a balanced and thorough portrayal of the organization and the people with whom he works. This point became clear to me some years ago when I told my wife about a complicated situation I was facing. The choice was whether or not to reorganize. Doing so meant demoting three people and the likely departure of two of them, both big contributors to revenue but poor managers. Not reorganizing would keep them (and the revenue they generated) at the company, but would perpetuate an ineffective structure and violate two values I had strongly endorsed: not allowing short-term revenue considerations to get in the way of doing the right thing, and, for managers at their level, greater emphasis on managing people well than on their own individual contributions.

My wife's response disappointed me because it reflected a one-dimensional view of the individuals involved, founded on details about their shortcomings that I had forgotten telling her. Her comments, though clear-headed, failed to take into account the value of the two individuals' contributions to the company. She didn't seem to understand that I wanted to eat my cake and have it too by finding a way to reassign them but keep them happy enough to stay. Eventually we traced her one-sided view to my tendency to talk to her about work only when I was frustrated. Like any sounding-board adviser, all she had to go on was what I had told her. Her counsel was disappointing because I had done an inadequate job as the advice taker.

Experts, experienced advisers, and sounding boards all occupy the high-priced seats, close to the action but nonetheless in the stands. The fourth kind of adviser is more intimately involved in the game the leader is trying to win.

The Partner Adviser

Partners differ from other advisers in three ways: the duration and intensity of their involvement, the way they employ tools and techniques, and their relationship with the leader.

Partnership Defined: Ongoing Involvement

Compared with other advisers, a partner puts in more time with the leader over a longer period. Experts are brought in only for the duration of a single project or to address a specific question. The leader typically turns to an experienced adviser in the early stages of his tenure or when coming to grips with a new problem. Sounding boards tend to be solicited sporadically, when the leader faces a dilemma or needs the perspective of a trusted outsider. The effectiveness of a partner, by contrast, depends on continuous involvement. Sometimes a partner adviser can be a colleague of the leader.

For example, a senior vice president of human resources is advising the COO, who is leading a process-improvement and cultural-change effort in the business units. Both report to the CEO and are peers in the senior management group. Because of the complexity and importance of the change effort, the HR head devotes most of his nonmanagerial time to serving as the COO's internal adviser, including attending staff meetings, traveling to plants and field offices, and facilitating off-site meetings. In other situations the partner adviser can be an outsider who has agreed to sign on part-time (perhaps a day or two a week) or full-time to help the leader for the duration of a change effort or the period when the new leader is taking hold.

Whether employee or outsider, a partner adviser gets to know both the leader and his organization well enough to understand the nuances of the culture and to predict what will work in a particular situation. For new leaders who do not know their subordinates well, and leaders whose subordinates have insufficient experience, an adviser in the role of partner can make all the difference. When Jack Welch became CEO of General Electric in 1981, he came to the job with a change agenda that would eventually transform the corporation. The following year Noel Tichy, a University of Michigan academic specializing in management development, signed on for twenty-four months to run the company's executive-development program, including its training center in Crotonville, New York. Welch needed a platform to communicate his vision of what GE had to become, and Crotonville became that platform. It also gradually became apparent to both Welch and Tichy that the changes Welch wanted to make called for a significant investment in training and education, including a new approach to developing executive talent. Because GE had always been a leader in management development, these changes had to be directed by someone who could win credibility for deep knowledge of other companies' training and development programs and for being on the leading edge of research in this area. He also had to immerse himself sufficiently to recognize the elements of GE's approach that should be retained while introducing new ways to challenge the company's managers. Tichy accepted the challenge. He never gave up his academic appointment, but jumped onto the playing field as a partner in the process of change that Welch wanted to pursue.

A Partnership in Action

Dirk became chairman and CEO of a health-care corporation after an eighteen-month planned transition. The company had been a mid-tier player in the industry when his predecessor, Tom, took over in the late 1970s. Over the next dozen years, Tom had transformed it by moving beyond domestic markets and by building the industry's best sales force. By the time Tom was ready to retire, the company was the worldwide market leader, the stock was at an all-time high, and Tom was revered by employees. He would be a hard act to follow.

Though the company was in the best shape ever, the marketplace had changed. Rapid expansion into foreign markets posed new challenges, and investment in the sales force had created an overhead structure that would be difficult to sustain without significantly more top-line growth. Dirk recognized that an acquisition was needed to supplement organic growth, and there also had to be an unprecedented level of cost control and efficiency. Managers were unaccustomed to spending limits, and integrating an acquisition would stress employees already handling more than ever before. Dirk faced a communication and motivation challenge. Some would question the need for an acquisition and cost containment and would resist changing habits that had produced unprecedented success. There were also political challenges: two people who reported to Dirk had expected his job and were angry about being passed over. He had made up his mind to replace them.

His main leadership challenges, he knew, were to acquire the right company, integrate it effectively, instill a new cost-consciousness, and win the loyalty of most of his direct reports while pressing the two disgruntled managers to retire as quickly and quietly as possible. Tom had managed the transition well, dealing with the board's concerns about Dirk. Because Tom had wanted the board to get to know Dirk as a future CEO, Dirk's previous two positions in the corporation had brought him into regular contact with the directors. Some found his style problematic. "He was aloof. Maybe it was arrogance, maybe he was just shy, but some of the directors just couldn't warm up to him," one said after Dirk was named CEO. "It made us wonder if he could win people's loyalty. People here loved Tom, the sales force in particular. And given how important they are to what the company has to do now, we wondered if he could win them over. But Tom told us Dirk was the guy for the job, so that was good enough for us."

Dirk looked for help. The adviser he turned to had counseled several executives in the company on strategy, organization, and operations problems and had gotten to know the organization well. He had also advised Dirk in his first corporate job several years before. This time he agreed to be available two or three days a week for eighteen months to offer counsel in two areas: (1) helping Dirk refine his image of a new culture and a plan to move toward it; and (2) helping Dirk align the senior executive group behind him, hold it accountable for realizing his vision, and ensure that managers who controlled important constituencies actively supported him.

Refining a Vision. Though a gifted general manager and businessman, Dirk was not introspective or attuned to others' reactions to him. He tended to believe that logic alone should convince people to change, but knew that logic would not persuade tens of thousands of managers and employees certain that they were living in the best of times that the company had to undergo difficult changes to stay successful. Dirk had to influence a critical mass of them to embrace change.

The plan that emerged from discussions and an exchange of white papers with the adviser called for sweeping changes, including how strategy would be set and expenses determined, how internal communication would be handled, and what would be expected of managers. The plan's centerpiece was a set of new behaviors for leaders and managers throughout the corporation, including changes in the hiring, development, and compensation systems. The specifics and implementation of these changes would be recommended to Dirk, the senior executive group, and the board of directors if necessary through several task forces made up of a cross-section of senior managers, and then communicated at a first-ever meeting of all senior and upper-level managers, who numbered in the hundreds.

Marshaling Political Support. To ensure political support, Dirk's adviser enlisted a senior executive (and possible future CEO) who was supportive of the changes Dirk wanted to make and the head of the largest division's sales force. The senior executive's role was to report to Dirk on the mood of the senior leaders and to influence them to support the change agenda. The sales VP could deliver credibility and the support of the powerful field sales organization. Along with the adviser, they formed an informal advisory group. An internal HR consultant was assigned to organize a series of meetings and coordinate corporate resources. It took several months of meetings with the core team, including a cross-section of upper-level managers, to produce a model of leader behaviors. The adviser organized the effort but stayed in the background to maximize the involvement of company executives so they would become committed to the results. He kept Dirk informed and pointed out when his presence could be most useful. Because it was well known that he was advising Dirk, he had access to key opinion leaders.

The meeting of senior managers would be most participants' introduction to the new CEO. It had two objectives: (1) to outline Dirk's vision for the company, explaining it as a work-in-progress that the managers would help to refine; and (2) to lay out the skills, behaviors, and attitudes that Dirk expected from them. Dirk and his three advisers recognized that the meeting's success depended on his ability to come across in a way that was not typical for him. His vision of how he wanted people to act was clear in Dirk's mind, but, as one of his people put it, "he doesn't know how to package it—how to get the message across in a way that people will get excited about it and want to do it." Another roadblock was his top team: An EVP, one of the aspirants to the CEO job, appeared to be lobbying his peers to resist Dirk's plan, and Dirk worried that he would use the meeting of senior managers as an opportunity to enlist them. "I have to get these people together, and now is the time to do it, but [the EVP] could really screw things up," Dirk said. "The last thing I need is for these people to see that we're not together as a team." The advisory group recommended that at the meeting each member of the top team be expected to describe some aspect of the leader-behavior model; thus none of them could distance himself from the plan.

Over the next two months, various groups helped prepare for the meeting while Dirk refined his vision in one-on-one conversations with the adviser. Each conversation was summarized in a white paper to keep development of the vision moving forward. Each paper also included comments on how Dirk could convey his message and examples of how other leaders had tackled a similar challenge.

The Culminating Event. The meeting was a bigger success than Dirk had hoped for. Positive reaction spurred HR to make overdue improvements in the performance-management system and in recruiting profiles for new managers. Dirk's vision of the company was received enthusiastically, and work-out groups during the meeting promoted a widespread sense of ownership. Dirk had worried about resistance to higher productivity goals, but the managers endorsed them. And though he did not discuss acquisitions, they agreed that the company needed more revenue growth quickly. "At least in my subgroup," one manager said in a plenary session, "everyone lined up behind the commitment to take on whatever we have to, to grow the top line." Then he addressed Dirk: "You and the board have to make this call, but we want you to know that we don't mind taking on more, or working harder, if that's what it's going to take. We're number one in the marketplace now, and we like how it feels. Staying on top is more important to us." Everyone cheered.

The EVP who lost out to Dirk participated fully in the meeting, but less enthusiastically than his peers. After the meeting he resisted Dirk less; a year later he retired. Dirk and the adviser continued to work together to ensure that the vision was reflected in the company's annual operating plans, in policies for hiring, promotion, and compensation, and in manager-development programs. They also worked on enhancing Dirk's team-development skills. Dirk had always viewed it as a leader's responsibility to identify problems and generate solutions for others to carry out. He began to understand that to motivate people at the most senior level, each of whom was a confident and experienced leader, he had to listen to their input and allow them to influence him. This meant that he had to reveal more of his thinking process to them along the way and ask for their help, as opposed to revealing only fully formed decisions. He also had to model a greater degree of openness if he expected them to reveal more about what they were thinking. One way he did so was by posting his own 360-degree feedback on the company intranet system, which caused the people on the top team to take their own feedback more seriously.

A Partnership's Concrete Benefits. What did Dirk gain from his advisory relationship? It had four benefits:

- A plan to launch his first era as CEO, including a way to gain widespread support for the changes needed at the company. Expectations and standards for the top tiers of managers were revised to align with Dirk's vision, and training programs were put in place to prepare people to meet them.

- Advice about an undertaking that his tenure as CEO depended on: sending a tough message of change while still building credibility with his managers, and doing so in a way that enlisted influential senior executives.

- Counsel from someone external to the organization and loyal to him who understood where he wanted to take the company, knew the organization, was trusted by senior managers, and could read the mood of the organization and advocate for Dirk's vision.

- Counsel on how to adjust his style—at this level, leadership styles don't change in fundamental ways—that increased his credibility, caused people to follow his lead rather than resist it, and helped set the stage for successful integrations of two large acquisitions.

What did Dirk do to gain these benefits? First, he recognized that the capability was lacking inside the company to provide the help he required. Second, he gave the adviser as much time and access as he needed without impinging on the other priorities in Dirk's schedule. Dirk told his administrative assistant, who controlled his calendar, about the adviser's work, which facilitated fitting in update meetings and getting material to Dirk promptly. Third, Dirk accepted feedback about his style, even though it had been good enough to win him the top spot. He understood that his behavior could be misinterpreted because few people in the company knew him well, and that because of the size of the organization he wouldn't learn of their reactions directly. Fourth, he tried out recommendations even if they were foreign to him. For example, he involved senior people whose loyalty he was unsure of in the change process. He also dealt with his political competitor by involving him more, rather than following his first impulse to isolate him. Dirk also worked at greater openness. He learned that explaining his assessment of the solution to a problem was only part of what his top team needed to hear from him. The other part was "But I'm not really sure what to do next here, and I need your help."

A mid-tier manager ascending the levels of the organization may require help in one or two categories—typically strategic and operational—but, on reaching the top job and embarking on a change effort, the leader suddenly experiences all four needs simultaneously. Each need is far more complex than he has ever faced before. Strategic decisions are tougher because the needs of the entire organization must be taken into account. Pressure to make strategic decisions often coincides with operational problems involving short-term cost, quality, and speed challenges. And the political and personal management skills that the top spot demands are often also unfamiliar. To coordinate all the parts of his organization, the leader must manage potentially volatile relationships to make the political environment work in his favor. All of these demands drain the leader's time and energy, increasing the risk that personal stress will compromise his ability to lead. Help is a must because of the complexity of the leader's tasks and because all four kinds of demands need attention simultaneously.

Can a single adviser provide the right capabilities in all four areas? No, at least not at the level of expertise needed by leaders who aim to change their organizations. Deep knowledge and experience are necessary to help meet intricate strategic, operational, and political needs. The best advisers will understand what each sphere requires, but they will have specialized in one or another in order to master its subtleties. Those who have been or are leaders themselves have experience to offer, but often it is limited to the particular set of conditions they faced. The leader facing tough complex challenges will be best served by nurturing a balanced network of advisers, representing different areas of specialty and made up of individuals well suited to his style and organizational needs.

CHAPTER **6**

The Art of Balance

I FIRST RECOGNIZED my own need for a balanced advice network in 1980, when one side of my firm was struggling while the other thrived. We had to shed some traditional businesses. Their impact had shrunk with the advent of next-generation approaches and innovations, but we had held on to them because they had helped create our franchise decades earlier. Meanwhile another of the company's businesses, the one I was most closely associated with, seemed to be on the verge of catching a wave. The CEO, my boss, had one foot in each camp. He had grown up in the company, and had run each of the traditional businesses during his rise to the top. But he also had the foresight to grasp, before anyone else in our industry, the potential power of merging the traditional parts of our business with the new part to create a capability that could produce unprecedented results for clients. The CEO was also managing another big change: a leadership handoff. He had made it plain that his successor would come from inside, and I was one of three candidates.

I was executive vice president, responsible for the quality and reliability function, industrial engineering, and the leadership and organization area, plus new-product development, automation, and several regional offices. We had created several of the early full-scale total-quality programs (the equivalent of today's Six Sigma) a few years before, and had formed one of the first just-in-time practices (today known as lean enterprise), an area that showed every sign of being a winner by the early 1980s. Transitioning to those principles and techniques and to the culture needed to sustain them, though, required our clients to have strong operational problem-solving abilities and equally strong organization-culture/people-development capabilities. They also had to adopt a business philosophy very different from what they were used to. By this time, the better-managed companies were beginning to realize that their existence would be in jeopardy if they did not make progress in each area.

We were leaders in introducing this new manufacturing and organizational model for three reasons: (1) We had an unmatched technical/operations lineage. We had created the first quality and reliability engineering service in 1946, invented material-requirements planning and, along with it, modern production and inventory control in 1958, and had helped lay the statistical process-control groundwork for variation management at Motorola, which eventually became the prototype Six Sigma program. (2) We understood the new philosophy. We had been affiliated with the Japanese Management Association for some time and had helped to introduce Japanese manufacturing methods into the United States. We had long-standing friendships with Edwards Deming and Joe Juran, the two statisticians most responsible for helping the Japanese create their manufacturing methodology. (3) We were experts in both aspects of what was necessary to make these models successful. We had deep expertise in leadership and culture change as well as operations, and had been the first consulting firm to successfully integrate both spheres into a single approach. We were in a great position in a rapidly expanding market, but we were not of one mind about what we wanted to become.

All of this took a toll on the people in the firm. The stress was high for a couple of reasons. First, the future of the company was at stake. We were at a strategic crossroads, and the wrong path would mean that the firm would soon lose momentum and decline or worse. Second, there was no mechanism within the firm to sort out our options or to handle the various perspectives, opinions, and emotions. People who reported to me and many outsiders encouraged me to take my part of the company and leave. But that choice would have affected everyone else in the company.

A Balanced Advice Network

I chose to see if the place could be turned around. I turned to three people for advice. What evolved over the next few years was my own balanced advice network.

Strategic Adviser:
An Expert and Experienced Practitioner

One adviser I turned to was Bruce Henderson, who had founded the Boston Consulting Group and originated strategy consulting. Bruce was a long-time friend of my firm.[1] I had met him because he was interested in the cross-disciplinary approach we had invented. Bruce retired from BCG around the time of our strategy inflection point and returned to his hometown of Nashville. He invited me to speak to a class he taught at the Owens Graduate Business School at Vanderbilt University, initiating a relationship that lasted for some time.

Bruce became my strategic adviser. We saw each other at least once every three months and typically talked through dinner and well into the early morning. His knowledge of the industry and of the kind of work my firm did—he had been head of purchasing at Westinghouse before joining A. D. Little—would alone have been useful. But he added the sharpest of strategic minds and relentless logic that forced me to think through our options as no one else had. Bruce challenged my assumptions constantly, sometimes Socratically, sometimes like a Talmudic teacher, and sometimes with a remark that showed me I wasn't as smart as I thought.

Bruce forced me to think strategically about a situation in which I was too emotionally entangled to maintain perspective. He taught me to look at options I wouldn't otherwise have considered about our practice and how the organization would have to change to get the most from it. Bruce also shared his own experience, first trying to change Arthur D. Little and then creating a firm with a unique mission. Both organizations became benchmarks for me. In the process, Bruce helped me clarify a new mental image of the place I wanted to create. He was prescriptive in his help to me: he had definite opinions about what would work and what would not, and he often defended a position forcefully. We debated fiercely. Bruce played the roles in my network of both expert and experienced adviser.

Political Adviser:
An Experienced Practitioner, Partner, and Sounding Board

My second adviser was Jim Richard, mentioned in chapter 5, who had studied under the psychotherapist Carl Rogers and served in Army Intelligence in Russia during World War II. Jim's exposure to Rogers's humanistic, nondirective form of therapy and firsthand experience of a culture that discouraged individual initiative inspired him to pursue management with a commitment to creating a work environment that would foster employee involvement and a productive competitive spirit. Eventually Jim became the CEO of a pump-manufacturing company in Iowa, where he was among the first clients of the people who had created the organization-development field (including Chris Argyris, Warren Bennis, Dick Beckhard, Bob Blake, Lee Bradford, and Jack Gibb).

Jim turned his company into an incubator where management and organization-development approaches that eventually became standard management practice were tested and nurtured. His advisers were also consulting to larger companies; one was Polaroid. One day Chris Argyris pointed out to Edwin Land, its founder and CEO, that Polaroid had reached the point of needing a more formal and professional approach to finding, managing, and motivating employees. Land asked where he should look. Argyris urged him not to hire someone in personnel—these were the days before it was called human resources—but to find an executive who had been in the top spot himself, responsible for making sure all the processes worked effectively. Jim Richard became the first head of human resources at Polaroid.

Jim's eclectic background equipped him with a sharp sense of organization culture and the politics that shape it; he was a wise and experienced observer of organizational life. I met him while I was still an undergraduate. We remained friends, and I eventually asked him to join the company as an in-house adviser. He understood what I wanted to create—it would build on what he had done—and I trusted him. I knew I could count on him for a deep grasp of the organization, partly because of his ability to get people to open up to him and partly because he understood the shadow organization. He was helpful when things went well, but particularly so when they were frustrating and the prospects of success bleak. Unlike Bruce, Jim did not offer opinions or solutions. Instead he pointed out aspects of the situations I was dealing with that enabled me to see what he saw, and pushed me to try to understand behavior that was frustrating me and the points of view of people I was trying to lead or influence. The give-and-take of our conversations produced influence and leadership strategies that we would continue to use over the next fifteen years.

The advice Jim provided was political. He functioned in part as an expert, because he had led his own organization through a time of change. But he was also my partner adviser, a role that encompassed functioning as my sounding board and directing projects within the firm to help me alter the culture.

Personal Adviser: A Sounding Board

My third adviser was Sandy Jenks, the long-time head of the counseling center at Boston College, whom I had known since my freshman year when he recruited me to attend a workshop to address the deteriorating climate on campus. (It was one of the earliest T-groups—the progenitor of today's team building—held on a college campus.) That workshop led to a campuswide program to reduce barriers between factions and train students and administrators in management and teamwork skills. Sandy, representing the administration and faculty, and I, as student director, were asked to start it.

Our programs and conflict-resolution projects seemed to succeed in reducing tensions and were soon recognized outside of the university. That led, in my sophomore year, to my first consulting project at a part of the State University of New York system. Others followed, at community-action agencies and universities. Because all this activity took the place of attending classes, I left at the end of my second year. For the next two years, I continued to do team-building and conflict-resolution work, and became a social worker running a boys' club in a small low-income city. Throughout this time Sandy kept track of me, and we got together whenever I was in Boston. He convinced me to return to college and, I'm sure, influenced the decision to readmit me. We then worked together to turn our original program into a group dynamics center (which still exists over thirty years later). Sandy and I remained friends after I graduated, and he regularly asked me to return to the campus to speak to groups of students and to catch up. He was interested in the work I was doing, but his questions more often focused on how satisfied I was with the professional course I had taken.

The advice Sandy provided me was personal, and the role he played in my network was as a sounding board. Sandy had spent his entire professional life as a teacher and counselor. Consulting, software, and the worlds of manufacturing, distribution, and financial services where I spent my time were foreign to him. But his detachment enabled him to be an effective sounding board and to focus on my well-being. When we met, I talked more about my frustrations with the pace of change than about the change itself. I might describe my satisfaction with a successful project rather than the details of the problem solving. Sandy became the only person with whom I opened up about what I was experiencing.

I gradually realized that talking to Sandy taught me to understand my reactions and to put things in perspective, skills that became particularly helpful when the company and I were both feeling the stress of change. After our conversations, I would feel more clearheaded about a path I had been uncertain about, or about what had caused the mistake I had made the day before—not because Sandy pointed it out, but because I had talked it through with someone who listened particularly well. Sandy was a trained counselor accustomed to talking to people who needed help. He knew how to ask questions and listen actively; he knew when to be quiet to draw me out and when to be direct and prescriptive. But those skills alone wouldn't have had such a profound impact on me were it not for the motivation behind them: he did not have to spend the time with me that he did—he was not paid to do it—but he was always available, out of sheer goodwill.

Prerequisites of a Balanced Advice Network

A strategic adviser who was both expert and experienced. A political expert who was an experienced adviser, a partner, and a sounding board. A personal adviser who was a sounding board. This is only one example of a balanced advice network. In my case it consisted of three people with very different personalities, abilities, and backgrounds, who did not know one another. I never brought them together as a team. Instead I formed a close relationship with each one, and all three relationships lasted a long time. I learned how fleeting such relationships could be, and how fortunate I had been, when all three died within a twelve-month period. The personal loss was difficult, and their friendships are irreplaceable. The professional loss was stunning; it took a long time to build a new network that came close to resembling that one.

What did I learn about taking advice from my experience with these three people? For one thing, I learned what I had to do to reap the most benefit from their help. If I kept my advisers informed between our face-to-face meetings, the time I spent with them was more fruitful. The optimal way to prepare for meeting Bruce was to perform my own analysis of what I faced, along with questions he could answer, often by laying out what he would do in my position. With Jim, it was preferable to describe in general terms what I wanted to see happen, or was trying to accomplish. Often he would think about it for a day or two and then return with a reaction that prompted me to recognize alternative approaches; then we would go back and forth on their pros and cons. Jim rarely said what he would do in my position unless I asked him directly. With Sandy, the key was willingness to talk openly and unguardedly. Simply talking about emotions with a friend I trusted was what mattered, and what eventually led to clarity.

Judging progress in working with advisers depends on the issues being addressed and the leader's needs. In my case, progress with Bruce was a matter of me addressing the complicated strategic dilemmas my company faced, which were the content of our discussions. It was also a function of how quickly I was able to envision a new course and lock onto a plan to move the company in that direction. Progress with Jim was measured by the degree and speed with which the company's culture changed for the better, and by my ability to balance the revenue and profit requirements with the emotional and developmental needs of my people. Progress with Sandy was a matter of me staying resilient and on an even keel emotionally. There are no generic systems to manage interactions with advisers. The best ways to do so depend on the situation and, in particular, on how the leader learns. In my own case, in addition to preparing for specific conversations, I kept a journal consisting mostly of notes about what had been discussed and reflections on our work. I also believe in the value of regular white papers or memos from the adviser summarizing major points discussed, posing new ideas to consider, or delving more deeply into a particular area.

FIGURE 6-1

Principles for a balanced advice network

Familiarity plus adaptability

Genuinely helpful advisers will have a demonstrated ability to adapt to the leader's situation and issues. They will be drawn from a pool of people whom the leader knows well enough to be certain that their style meshes with his or hers.

Relationship potential

The greatest benefit will emerge from a relationship in which the leader and the adviser genuinely want to work with each other. The importance of the relationship to his or her success makes it essential for the leader to sharpen his or her relationship-building skills.

Shared management but sole responsibility

The leader and the adviser share responsibility for building and maintaining a good relationship. It is the leader's responsibility to manage the network and the adviser's to make it easy for the leader to do so.

Getting the most from an advice network is not unlike managing any other relationship. It must evolve, adapting over time to changing conditions, and it must be resilient enough to weather setbacks. The leader must think through what he wants to gain and how to judge progress, and he must put effort into nurturing the relationships. Also, there must be a system in place to keep things moving so that the leader and his advisers can communicate easily when necessary. When these tasks are approached from the advice taker's point of view, three general principles for a balanced advice network emerge.

Familiarity Plus Adaptability

The participants in an enduring and vibrant advice network become deeply familiar with the leader's decision-making and learning styles, and with his values. But familiarity is not enough for a relationship to endure. Advisers must also be able to adapt to the unpredictable conditions the leader faces, or even to anticipate them. Adaptable advisers will always be on the lookout for better ways to handle what the leader faces in the realms they know best. And a wise advice taker will make adaptability a primary criterion when choosing advisers.

Advice takers who treat the familiarity and comfort of an existing relationship as more important than adaptability tend to benefit less from their advisers over time. Rita, whom we met in chapter 2, made this mistake when she chose as advisers family friends who were unfamiliar with the kind of company hers had become. Other leaders stick with advisers who do not adapt to changing conditions. An example is Eric, the second-generation owner of a family company. Eric took pride in the company's long-standing relationships with its raw-materials suppliers, some of which harked back to the company's founding. His advice-taking mistake was to approach relationships with advisers the same way. When a divestiture opportunity arose, one that Eric had to move on quickly, he turned to the company's attorney without considering whether other law firms could provide better help. The attorney promised to get back to him right away. Two weeks passed; when Eric called again, the attorney said he'd been compiling information and needed a few more days. Two more weeks passed. Finally Eric realized that the attorney had never dealt with such a transaction but did not want to say so to a long-time client. There is no excuse for such behavior, but ultimately Eric was at fault for retaining an unqualified adviser because he was a known quantity.

Adaptable advisers demonstrate an ongoing ability to challenge the leader's thinking and to foster well-considered decisions, even in unfamiliar situations. One leader said that she keeps using advisers "who help me come up with creative solutions to what I'm dealing with. They have a way of making me think differently about something. They ask questions that the people who report to me don't ask, and they put things in a way that helps me see what I'm dealing with from a different angle."

Good advice takers don't just find flexible advisers; they construct flexible networks, embodying the best combination of skills to meet particular needs. In the opening scene of the classic television series *Mission Impossible*, the leader of the clandestine spy group, Mr. Phelps, listened to a taped description of the situation while reviewing agents' dossiers and chose a team whose combined skills and temperaments met the unique needs of the assignment. Similarly, the right advisers will possess the knowledge, experience, and/or expertise needed for the kinds of challenges the leader faces and a demonstrated ability to adapt to his situation and time demands. They will be people whom the leader has gotten to know well enough to believe that their styles jibe well with his. Once that match is made, the next requirement is a strong working relationship.

Relationship Potential

A bond of some sort between leader and adviser is a prerequisite for a collaborative relationship to form. It might arise from mutual respect, or the adviser's admiration for the leader's vision, or the kind of challenging back-and-forth that produces one-plus-one-equals-three results. Whatever the reason, the leader and adviser must genuinely want to work together.

From the leader's point of view, basic prerequisites for choosing a particular adviser are enough trust to be willing to open up and enough respect to actively seek the adviser's opinion. And the leader should feel certain that the adviser wants to work with him. One test for the external adviser who does this work for a living is whether an ongoing relationship with the leader is compelling for reasons other than the fee it will generate. Any professional relationship depends on fair compensation, but help of the intensity this book advocates requires motivation beyond the routine desirability of an advisory fee. Providing the right help consistently calls for attention, diligence, and energy to match the leader's intensity and drive to succeed; the adviser will have less at stake than the leader, but should be ready to expend effort commensurate with what the leader has at stake. In other words, the adviser must be sufficiently committed to the leader and to what he has set out to accomplish to go the extra mile consistently.

Some types of advice and some advisory roles depend more than others on a deep collaborative relationship. A relationship with a personal adviser calls for deeper trust and more similarity of sensibilities than does a relationship with a strategic adviser. Because a political adviser often delivers tough feedback—about how the leader has provoked employees' hostility, for example, or how his behavior is sabotaging his efforts—that relationship demands more openness than a relationship with an operational adviser. Its tone and content, however, differ from the emotional intimacy of a relationship with a personal adviser. Similarly, the advice of experts and experienced advisers is usually less personally strenuous than that of sounding-board and partner advisers. A solid relationship is also important to those who shoulder the role of personal adviser, whose willingness to do so is driven by their commitment to the leader and a deep desire to help.

Both parties in the relationship participate in forming and nurturing it. But it is the leader's relationship-building abilities that will determine whether he receives what he needs from his advice network. Ideally, he will be self-aware enough to recognize how his behavior helps or hinders openness. He must be frank in revealing his objectives and worries, their importance to him, and the importance of his work with the adviser. And he must be perceptive enough to pick up cues that the adviser is willing to go beyond the letter of their agreement to provide whatever help is needed.

There are three messages for the leader: (1) You will feel more comfortable, and get more out of the collaboration, if you choose advisers you genuinely want to work with. (2) Make sure your advisers are comparably eager to work with you, and are not just pursuing revenue or building up their résumés. (3) Work on sharpening your relationship-building abilities, and select the type of relationship that best suits the type of advice you need and the roles your advisers will play in the network. In my experience, leaders who have trouble building solid long-term relationships tend to have unbalanced advice networks.

Shared Management but Sole Responsibility

It is up to both parties in an advice relationship to maintain regular contact and a constant flow of relevant information, even when the adviser is not actively working on a task for the leader. Doing so enables the leader to step back from the preoccupations of the moment to survey the status of the longer-term agenda with someone knowledgeable and plugged-in but a step removed from the immediate issues. Intermittently bringing advisers up to date on his progress also enables them to be helpful faster when the need arises again for their direct involvement.

Given the demands on the leader's time, advisers must expect to accommodate to the leader's schedule by making themselves available at his convenience rather than their own. Advisers should also help the leader make the most efficient use of their time together by asking the questions and proposing the mechanisms that best enable the leader to make progress on his agenda. Depending on the leader's style of learning and decision making, these mechanisms could be as simple as a short memo prior to a scheduled conversation in which the adviser tees up the issues and questions he considers most pertinent. Some leaders prefer the give-and-take of conversation to reach clarity on a course of action. In these cases, the adviser might offer to write up a summary of their discussion, highlighting its most salient points, to maintain a record of major decisions and follow-up items and to conserve the leader's time. Indeed, one way for the leader to determine whether to continue to work with particular advisers is to ask himself if they have facilitated communication and taken initiative to make it easier for him to do what he must.

Thus both leader and adviser should share the task of managing the relationship. But when it comes to putting a balanced advice network in place and making sure it fulfills its purpose, the responsibility is the leader's alone. He has the most to gain or lose. And only he can decide which advisers to talk to, when to talk with them, and how the network should operate to best meet his needs. This principle has two parts: (1) The leader and the adviser share the task of ensuring that their relationship is fruitful and meets the leader's needs. (2) It is the leader's responsibility to manage the network, and the adviser's to make it easy for the leader to do so.

The Primacy of the Advisory Relationship

To add real value to a helping relationship, more is required than the right background, the right experience, and even the right knowledge and skills. Advisers also need the kind of interpersonal capabilities that will foster a strong and positive relationship with the leader. Why is the relationship so important?

For three reasons: (1) The adviser's approach must be tailored to the unique strategic, operational, and political conditions each leader faces. There is no formula; the right answer will emerge from a melding of the leader's outlook and his advisers'. The better the relationship, the more likely it is that multiple approaches will be vetted and combined. (2) The leader needs advice that is actionable—advice that the leader, with his strengths, shortcomings, and limitations, can successfully execute. To fully understand his capacity to turn advice into action, the leader must be willing to engage in open dialogue about personal preferences, strengths, shortcomings, and constraints. The stronger the relationship, the franker and more open the dialogue. (3) The leader is entering unknown territory. Once he selects advisers, trust is a bedrock condition if he is to follow the route they suggest, or even to explore and debate those suggestions and eventually hammer out agreement.

Many smart, experienced, knowledgeable, and dedicated people offer advice, but without the ability to build strong, collaborative relationships with those whom they advise, they will not be great at it. Regardless of specialty, background, or reputation, best-in-class advisers—those who are best at truly helping—have the skills to build effective working relationships with leaders who possess different backgrounds and capabilities. These advisers create relationships in which their own abilities fit into those of the leader like pieces of a puzzle. When this happens, the adviser gets the right points across, and does so in a way that matches how the leader learns. He influences in a way the leader responds to. Their conversations are easy; the adviser's question elicits a response, and the adviser's reply builds on it in a way that prompts the leader to mention something he might not otherwise have thought of. The fluidity of communication sparks new ideas. These are the signs of a productive and creative relationship, whose two participants are working together because they genuinely want to.

Do I Want to Work with This Person?

Four capabilities are basic in a helping relationship with a leader: adaptation, listening, feedback, and empathy.

FIGURE 6-2

Relationship-building capabilities to look for in an adviser

Adaptability

Listening

Feedback

Empathy

Adaptability

An adaptable adviser tailors what he offers and how he does so to the leader's situation and learning style. Adaptability saves the leader time and makes it easier for him to concentrate on priorities. If, for example, a leader's time demands preclude long meetings, his advisers must accommodate their agendas to shorter interactions. If he learns best by reading and pondering the issues and options before discussing them, it is up to his advisers to tee up their key questions and analyses in written form, clearly and concisely enough to be self-explanatory. Often a leader with such a style benefits from receiving a short white paper before meeting with an adviser, and a written summary afterward. If the leader learns best through give-and-take conversation and debate, the adviser must adjust accordingly, perhaps honing his influence and communications skills. Professional consultants are likely to have acquired this kind of adaptability in the course of dealing with multiple clients, but it is incumbent on internal advisers as well, especially those who lend assistance to a new leader.

Listening

A skilled adviser listens carefully enough to grasp the scope of the leader's intentions, perceptively enough to understand why they matter to him, and presciently enough to anticipate their potential ramifications and outcomes. The adviser's listening skill is fundamental to accurate interpretation of the leader's intent and accurate translation of the leader's vision and objectives into actions. Because a leader can be so close to a situation that he fails to see inconsistencies, gaps, oversights, or looming problems, skillful advisers practice what the psychotherapist Erich Fromm called "listening with a third ear"—listening for what the leader is not saying but should be addressing. Depending on the situation, this kind of perceptiveness can provide the leader a new perspective ("I hadn't thought about it that way") that may enable him to generate new options.

Feedback

Listening effectively enough to recognize subtleties that the leader has missed is only of value to the relationship if the adviser is also skilled at delivering substantive feedback effectively. Another function of well-honed feedback is to convey to the leader how he comes across to others. The leader should look for an adviser who can point out shortcomings in his behavior in a way that promotes insight without activating defensiveness. When the leader fails to learn from feedback, the fault usually lies in the adviser's failure to adhere to the principles of effective feedback: that it be well timed, that it match the leader's needs and learning style, that it be backed up with examples, that it address something he can change, and that it be free of the adviser's biases.

Empathy

Finally, skilled advisers have a well-developed capacity for empathy—awareness of the leader's feelings, thoughts, and experiences, even when the leader does not explicitly describe them. Empathy is important to the relationship because the leader will reveal more if he believes he is understood, thus offering the adviser more to work with. Empathy on the part of the adviser is also a tool in stress management: the more the leader reveals about the origins of his frustration or anger, the greater the chances of alleviating the stress that goes hand in hand with bringing about change.

Adaptation, listening, feedback, and empathy are not specific to a particular type of advice or kind of advisers. These skills are just as important for the expert, who must impart knowledge in such a way that the leader grasps it efficiently, as they are for the partner who participates directly in the change process. They are as important to an adviser–leader relationship that concentrates on strategy as they are to a joint effort to take on the politics of the shadow organization. Every combination is built on a relationship; the better it is, the more the leader will benefit.

This chapter has described the architecture of a balanced advice network. A seam running through it and previous chapters is that it is the responsibility of the leader to ensure that he receives the advice that will help him most. Exercising that responsibility depends on the leader's mind-set about help and about being an advice taker, and on how he behaves as he solicits and manages advice.

CHAPTER 7

Attitudes and Behavior of Great Advice Takers

UNDERSTANDING TYPES OF ADVICE and kinds of advisers, and knowing how to judge advisers' abilities to form relationships, are stage-setting skills. Even with the most talented advisers, getting the best help requires the leader to be fully engaged in the relationship and to manage it skillfully. Full engagement and skillful management depend on both attitudes and behavior.

Attitudes

What attitudes foster successful management of a helping relationship? Three sets of attitudes are most decisive:

- Willingness to take responsibility and to be receptive

- Inquisitiveness and openness to new ideas

- Commitment to self-awareness and acceptance of feedback

Responsibility and Receptivity

"I've used advisers of all different types, a lot of them," one leader told me. "Some I've gone out to look for, because I had a big problem we couldn't solve. Some I've looked up to keep a problem from happening. And some came to me to sell something. But whichever way they get here, the project still has to start with that person and me looking each other in the eyes and agreeing on what he's going to do and what I'm going to do. Whenever I haven't taken that step, I've regretted it. Things just seem to get screwed up if it doesn't happen."

What does he do, I asked, if he is unsure what the issues are at the outset? "Then we keep talking about it until it is clear. But it's my responsibility to keep bringing it up, and to push it until it's clear. It's probably an advantage to the adviser to keep it fuzzy, but it's an advantage to me to get it clear. So I do it and don't expect the adviser to." He summarized his responsibility this way:

> It comes down to a handful of things. First, I have to be feeling some pain somewhere that hurts enough for me to do something about it. Maybe it's a strategy that we shouldn't have pursued, but we're locked in. Or a couple of sales divisions are way under plan for the first time and we can't figure out why. My part of this is to say "It hurts over here." I don't know why it's hurting, but I have to describe why it's a problem that it hurts. I also have to know what success looks like—not necessarily with a lot of precision, but I'm the one who should say, "If this thing gets solved, here's what it's going to be like around here." If I don't do that, there's no target, no end state that we can aim at. "Ends and means" is not a bad way to put it. My job is the ends, the adviser's job is how to get there.

He also mentioned a third responsibility that was his alone. "I have to have a way to know whether there's progress—to measure where we are and how far we have to go. Sometimes that comes down to talking to people, and getting the sense of progress that way, other times we should have formal progress reviews. But here again, I have to be clear about what works for me."

This leader told me that what got him up in the morning was awareness that a problem would go unsolved if he didn't tackle it. The same embrace of responsibility comes through in his role as a client. "If I don't get the right advice," he said, "it's probably because I didn't do something right. I'm the one responsible for how much of the right help I get."

A leader willing to assume responsibility for a relationship with an adviser may be demanding, but he does not expect the adviser to do all the heavy lifting. The best advice takers assume ownership of the process in the same way that they assume responsibility for the culture and the financial performance of their organizations. They take on what they must, and make it clear what they expect of their advisers. Those who don't embrace this attitude expect the adviser to take on assignments that belong to the leader alone, such as defining the outcome of a change effort or envisioning the future behavior of the organization. Advisers can help by offering a model for visioning, offering up ways to define the right strategies, raising the right questions, and providing tools. But the role of advisers is to provide the means to arrive at ends that are defined by the leader.

By definition, the most basic barrier to great advice taking is refusal to accept help when it is necessary. I am not referring to thinking carefully about a piece of advice and rejecting it because it seems off-target; I mean failing to seek or accept help even after recognizing that it is needed. Why do some leaders resist being influenced while others, equally accomplished, are receptive?

"It's probably because of insecurity," said the general counsel of a large corporation, to whom I posed this question. "The ones who resist the ideas of others have to believe they're right, and know everything they need to know. Allowing yourself to be influenced is admitting you don't know everything." A senior HR manager speculated: "It comes down to which concept of leading they have. The one where the leader tells everyone what to do and expects them to do it; they tend to only care that their answer is the one that is accepted. Or the leader who wants people to have a say and is willing to share the responsibility; they just want the right answer and don't mind if it comes from someone else." A third person, a psychotherapist, said: "Some people respond to power by letting their arrogant side overcome their humble side. They believe they know better than anyone else what has to happen. One way the arrogant side and the humble side get out of balance is when something bad happens that is out of their control. And when it is something someone warned them about that they ignored, they get embarrassed, feel guilt, and get stubborn."

An unusually high need for control was cited by several people. One described a talented subordinate he had hired. "I thought he was going to be my backup. This guy had everything going for him, but he only lasted a year and a half. He had his way of doing things, and just wouldn't recognize that he needed to adapt a little bit to our way of doing things. I had the HR head and the CFO talk to him, and I tried to give him feedback, and his division HR guy tried to get him to be more flexible. He'd seem to pay attention, but he just couldn't let go. Then we did a 360-degree feedback, and the big message was that his people and peers were starting to write him off because he had his game plan and wouldn't listen to anyone's ideas. This is a guy who just has to have things done his way, and doesn't really care about how other people see it. That's why he's not here anymore."

Several people used the term *narcissistic* to describe people who are not open to influence. This basic personality type, first identified by Sigmund Freud, is associated with people who gravitate to leadership roles, push for changes to their societies and organizations, and attract followers in a charismatic way. But Michael Maccoby, writing about the negative side of narcissism, points out that because narcissists are extremely self-absorbed and self-protective, they must be convinced that they can benefit personally before accepting help. They tend to listen only for what they want to hear because of preconceived notions about what is best for them. Narcissists are also overly sensitive to criticism, and don't listen when they believe they are being criticized. They lack empathy, which becomes a barrier to communication.[1] Carl Rogers pointed out that empathy is a key to successful relationships because it enables us to listen with understanding and to be open to other people's views.[2]

Refusal to be influenced may arise from narcissism, a need to be seen as right, arrogance, high control needs, or a mixture of these traits. The bottom line is that a leader facing tough problems who ignores available help is abdicating responsibility and letting down those who depend on his stewardship.

Inquisitiveness and Openness to New Ideas

Smart advice takers are open to new ways of looking at things and eager to learn from any source. They tend to be on the alert for useful input in all their interactions. One sign of this attitude is the absence from the leader's vocabulary of phrases like, "We don't have much to learn about that. We do a better job than anyone else," or "This doesn't really apply to us, because our business is different."

A setting in which inquisitiveness and an open mind are particularly conspicuous is benchmarking trips. There are two kinds of benchmarking. In one scenario, a consultant or junior staff member gathers data on another company to try to understand its capabilities. In the more active and illuminating kind of benchmarking, people from one organization visit another to observe firsthand something that it does particularly well. Here's what happened on one such trip.

The vice chairman of a large health-care company, convinced that his organization had to become leaner and more efficient, convened a team of high-potential midlevel managers to make recommendations. Among their suggestions was to visit leading suppliers of components to computer manufacturers. The team pointed out to those who were skeptical about looking at another industry, including most of the company's senior managers, that these component suppliers had faced customer demands very similar to their own company's. The suppliers that had captured the biggest share of the computer-component market, furthermore, were those that had become most efficient and adopted the most innovative customer-interaction practices. The vice chairman overruled the senior managers' objections and instructed the analysis group to arrange visits.

Six managers visited a leading component supplier, a much smaller enterprise than the health-care corporation. After a tour of the facilities and an overview of the manufacturing process, the health-care group split up into functional pairs to meet with their counterparts from the host company. The two sales executives, Sam and Olivia, met with the head of sales and his deputy. Sam, a thirty-year veteran, was fiercely loyal to the company and knew only its style and practices. Olivia was a rising star who had joined the marketing department after receiving an MBA and had recently moved to sales. After a two-hour session with the head of sales and his deputy, Sam and Olivia joined the others from the health-care company to recap the day. Sam reported that their hosts were pleasant but that he had heard nothing transferable to their company. "Nothing to learn here, really," he said. "We could have spent this time more productively calling customers."

Someone asked Olivia if she had anything to add. Though careful to express respect for Sam, she said, in effect, that she could not disagree more about the transferability of what they had heard. She described in detail a customer-service philosophy quite different from their own in its emphasis on the customer's point of view. Customer-service people at the components supplier, she said, believed that customers considered them the most important part of the company, which made them work hard to anticipate customer needs. And she noted that they were often singled out for recognition awards, a foreign practice at their own company where customer-service jobs were entry-level and little training was provided.

Olivia spoke for about ten minutes. When she finished, someone joked that Sam must have attended a different meeting. After dinner an embarrassed Sam approached Olivia and wondered aloud why he had picked up none of what she learned. Though Sam's question was addressed more to himself than to her, Olivia observed that he had asked no questions at the meeting. Sam said he had been unaware of that. He acknowledged that her observations could help their company as long as they were transferable to their larger, more structured environment. They decided to use the second meeting with their hosts to discuss how to transfer particular practices.

This is not a case of a stubborn long-term employee consciously rejecting good ideas out of loyalty to his own company. Nor was Sam upset that a smaller company had come up with better practices. He was telling the truth when he said that he had not heard what Olivia had. Why had he listened so selectively? Perhaps he was such a salesman at heart that his impulse to influence his hosts, to make the sale, overpowered his need to learn. Or perhaps he had simply made up his mind that he was not going to hear anything useful.

It is not uncommon for lack of inquisitiveness and openness to new ideas to go hand in hand with another trait that gets in the way of advice taking: lack of self-awareness.

Self-Awareness and Acceptance of Feedback

Self-awareness is a must for a leader seeking to benefit from advice. In this practical sense of the term, self-awareness has two components: recognition of his own strengths and shortcomings, and awareness of his own emotions and their impact on judgment and decision-making performance. Openness to feedback is an unmatched route to greater self-awareness.

Recognizing personal strengths and shortcomings requires an honest appraisal of our records and accomplishments. It can also sometimes call for reining in our goals. Take the case of Richard, a talented manager respected by his peers and subordinates. The division Richard ran was outside the corporation's mainstream business, and as a result rarely received the financial or political support Richard considered necessary to grow revenue and profit. But his hard work and dedication were recognized by the CEO and by the EVP to whom he reported. When the company decided to sell Richard's division, he was offered another position at the same level. He turned it down and left the corporation. Richard later came close to one CEO offer, but could not find a position running anything larger than the division he had managed. Two years later, after his severance and health-care benefits had expired, he was still without a job. Why did this happen?

Richard had set his sights too high. He held out for a bigger job than those that were available to him. Because he was a skilled manager with a good record who interviewed well, he was offered two positions but turned down both. "I know I can get something bigger," he said. "I'm good enough to be a CEO of a smaller company or a COO of a large one." Call it delusions of grandeur, an inflated ego, refusal to face reality, or overconfidence. Whatever the label, Richard held onto a self-image out of keeping with how those with jobs to offer viewed him and his abilities.

Several executive-search consultants told Richard that his sights were set too high and encouraged him to consider positions like the last one he had held. If he did so, they predicted, he would soon have several to choose from. But he refused to see that his aspirations were unrealistic. He viewed his capabilities as he wished them to be, rather than in terms of his actual and probably future accomplishments. A person of sound judgment when it came to running a business, Richard put the brakes on his own career because he was not honest with himself.

Becoming more self-aware also helps advice takers understand the role that emotions play in behavior and decision making. There is value in recognizing the groundswell of anger that arises when one's judgment is questioned, or the frustration of seeing no reasonable route to where one wants to go. Tracing the link between anger or frustration and intemperate remarks can be a springboard to paying closer attention to how one communicates. And self-awareness also helps a leader monitor whether emotions are dictating his behavior in a particular situation. Self-aware leaders recognize an emotional reaction as soon as it begins to take hold and figure out how to express or harness or deflect it productively.

Emotions reflect values and core beliefs, and sometimes they signal feelings about long-standing unresolved issues. Our behavior and the decisions we make in the grip of strong emotions can hurt our chances of success. Consider Claude, a former corporate division president who had been passed over for promotion. The blow to his ego and pride prompted him to leave abruptly. Claude joined a privately owned company in the same industry, one with a fraction of the volume and financial resources he was used to, persistent quality problems, an untrained workforce, and managers unequal to the task of growing the business. Claude eventually became chairman, CEO, and primary owner. The company never seemed to have enough money to invest in technology, equipment, or people. Particularly vexing were the flat productivity and product-quality problems of the manufacturing plant. Claude's stress provoked outbursts of pent-up frustration, often aimed at the operations staff. A board member pointed out that Claude was frustrated because the company's problems were concentrated in manufacturing, where he lacked expertise. The board member encouraged Claude to hire as EVP-Operations a capable manager, Miles, who had worked for him at his previous company.

Miles quickly imposed basic controls, imported quality practices, made visible supervisory changes, and injected a new spirit into the company. His competence enabled Claude to concentrate on customer relations, which he did well. Thanks to Miles's operational improvements, the business began to make money and gain market share. Miles's influence with Claude increased. Eventually he began giving Claude feedback about the impact of his outbursts on morale and thus on the pace of improvements in the plant. Miles carefully avoided provoking a defensive outburst, but he was persistent.

As the value of the company grew, the board embarked on a strategy review and decided to sell the company. A large international corporation seeking a foothold in the United States emerged as a potential buyer. After due diligence began, Claude complained that the chairman of the corporation had not contacted him. It was arranged that Claude would visit the corporation's European headquarters to meet the chairman. The meeting went badly: the chairman arrived late, and by the time they were introduced little time remained. Feeling slighted, Claude declared that the European company's offer was too low and that he was pulling the company off the market.

Two years passed. Miles's improvement efforts made the company an outstanding performer in the industry. Eventually Miles became Claude's primary internal political adviser, and he also played the role of partner adviser, the person to whom Claude listened most carefully about his behavior. Miles's counsel made all the difference in how this story ends. Slowly, Claude's self-awareness grew. He came to recognize the continuum between his emotions and his behavior well enough to recognize danger signs. If strong feelings began to overtake him, he would defer to Miles, or Miles would recognize the signs and take over. When the company was again put up for sale. Claude handled himself quite differently during negotiations. The company was sold at an attractive price.

The examples of Richard and Claude underline the indispensability of both self-awareness and openness to feedback. They also suggest an important success factor: ability to accept what one learns about oneself, even if it is painful. It is the job of the adviser to point out the connection between weaknesses and mistakes and what the leader wants to achieve. It is the leader's job to look hard at the occasionally unattractive reflection in the mirror, accept it, and learn from it.

Behavior

Responsibility, receptivity, openness, and self-awareness set the foundation for effective advice taking, but the right attitudes alone are not enough. The other ingredient is a particular way of behaving and some interpersonal skills that enable the leader to turn attitudes into action through two vital steps: choosing the right help and building an advice network. Deciding on the right type of help begins with analyzing the existing situation, envisioning an ideal state, and pinpointing the needs for which help is necessary. Then the objective is to construct the optimal configuration of advisers by selecting the right people and forming solid relationships with them.

FIGURE 7-1

Attributes and abilities of a skilled advice taker

Attitudes	Behavior
Willingness to take responsibility and to be influenced	Selecting the right kind of help
• Responsibility for what only a leader can do	• Analysis of the situation
• Recognition of self-imposed blocks to being influenced	• Force field analysis
	• Compilation in written form, and reviewed by a trusted aide
	• Matching needs with specific types of help and kinds of advisers
Inquisitiveness and openness to new ideas	
• Lack of insistence that "our business is different"	• Managing expectations
• Careful, unbiased fact-seeking	• Matching learning and decision-making styles
	Constructing a network
Commitment to self-awareness	• Selection
• Realization of strengths and shortcomings	• Content
• Awareness of emotions	• Competence
	• Chemistry
	Establishing relationships
	• Practicality
	• Added value
	• Dependability
	• Commitment

Selecting the Right Kind of Help

The first step is to assess the current situation as thoroughly as possible, honestly acknowledging the organization's shortcomings, including those of its people and their interactions, the political climate, and the impact of various coalitions.

The next step is to specify how the ideal company would differ from what exists today. What would the leader overhear as she passes a group of managers discussing an important project? If a senior-level person were being recruited for an important post, how would the leader want the candidate to feel while visiting the facility and being interviewed? What kinds of people would be members of the senior management group? How would they collaborate? What would the organization structure look like? If a customer were unhappy, how would the organization respond? This ideal image could be written up or talked through with an adviser; the leader could generate it on her own and then present it for reactions, or it could emerge from a give-and-take discussion. It depends on the leader's style and what works best for her.

A leader facing an operational challenge should begin with a description of what is working and what is not. Then he should try to describe in equivalent detail the ideal situation, in which the current problem has been solved and opportunities are captured. Many leaders find the current situation easier to describe than the ideal, since they are unsure what is possible. This in itself is a valuable discovery; once the leader presents his analysis to his advisers, it will point them in a direction where they can provide useful input.

Once the "is" and the "should be" are sketched out, the final analytical step draws on a seminal tool of social-system analysis developed by the psychologist Kurt Lewin.[3] In the aftermath of World War II Lewin hypothesized that world conflicts could be understood by borrowing vector theory from mathematics. Relationships between groups of people, Lewin asserted, are subject to forces (vectors) that exert influence in different directions. If the mass of the forces pushing in one direction equals that of forces pushing in the other direction, the situation will not change. But if one side gains power—by adding or strengthening forces or by eliminating forces on the other side—the situation will be pushed in one direction or the other.

A simple four-step *force-field analysis* can be a useful way to conceptualize the problems facing an organization:

1. Speculate on the forces that hinder the organization from moving closer to the ideal. They might include people who lack needed capabilities, inadequate financial resources, a strategy inappropriate to the ideal the leader envisions, or a culture that discourages desired behavior.

2. Assign two values to each obstructive force: one signifying the magnitude of its contribution to hindering progress, and the other representing the difficulty of eliminating it or mitigating its influence.

3. Identify the forces that exert influence in a positive direction, pushing the organization toward its ideal. Here too, these forces may include skills, financial resources, attitudes, or structures.

4. Assign each of these facilitating forces a value signifying its relative importance in moving the organization toward its ideal and a value representing its strength.

This evaluation will identify hindering forces that must be eliminated or disabled for progress to be made. It will also pinpoint those that it is realistic to change, and the facilitating forces that can be counted on to push the organization forward from where it is to where it could be. In a cash-strapped company struggling to develop innovative products, for example, it may not be realistic to expend a lot of energy on a hindering factor like "lack of investment funds for R&D," despite its importance. But a factor like "a marketing-to-distribution process that is too cumbersome and bureaucratic," though of moderate importance compared to investment funds, is more feasible to correct. Both sets of insights will help determine the types of advice and kinds of advisers that can be of most help. It is wise to write up this analysis. A written version is likely to be more detailed and more objective than a casual scratch-pad version, and a written analysis can also be critiqued.

In fact, someone the leader trusts should review the analysis for oversights. If Barry, whom we met in chapter 2, had taken this simple step, it might have made all the difference. His analysis overemphasized matters he was already comfortable with at the expense of the areas where he actually needed the most help. Had Barry just consulted a trusted friend, someone who knew his strengths and shortcomings, he might have seen the pitfall ahead of him in time.

The next task is to find the right people to help. This step has two parts: (1) using the written analysis to identify the kinds of help needed, and (2) making sure that help is tailored to how the leader learns and based on clearly defined expectations about the kinds of people he wants to advise him.

Deciding on the Configuration of Help. By pinpointing the forces that are both important and realistic to address, a well-executed force-field analysis will clarify the mix of strategic, operational, political, and personal advice that is needed and will help to determine their sequence.

If the leader is new both to a top-level job and to the organization, a strategy expert who knows the industry may be particularly helpful. If extensive organizational change is called for, an adviser who is both a strategic thinker and experienced at culture change is imperative. Not only can the right operational adviser help achieve financial targets through cost savings and efficiencies, he can also help build the new leader's credibility by ensuring that these advantages are realized quickly. If the organization has political problems, like people jockeying for the leader's favor or constant conflict between top-team members (particularly serious for a leader in a new position, but also likely to happen when an in-place leader changes his organization), it would be wise to find a political adviser. If the leader is under intense pressure and has no one with whom to talk in confidence, a personal adviser who provides a safe harbor—someone who can be trusted implicitly—is an important addition to the advice network. Because the onset of stress is unpredictable for a leader seeking change, however, it is wise to nurture a relationship with a personal adviser before stress makes such a relationship urgent.

The leader's situation and style determine the most appropriate mix of advisers in his network. If he faces a new competitive or operational situation with many unknowns, an expert and/or experienced adviser is probably needed. If the challenge is to change the organization in a fundamental way, he will be well served by finding a partner adviser.

Matching Learning Styles and Expectations. Different people learn differently. Howard Gardner of the Harvard Graduate School of Education and Boston University School of Medicine asserts that intelligence does not have a single uniform definition; it consists of a broad spectrum of abilities and proclivities. People also learn in different ways, Gardner says, and success at doing so is a matter of finding one's preferred way to learn. David Kolb's research also explores differences in how people grasp skills and ideas, and his learning-styles theory can help leaders who are constructing advice networks. Each of us, Kolb said, has a distinctive learning style dominated by two or three of these four distinct ways of learning:

- *Concrete experience.* People who learn best this way pursue understanding through personal experience. These are the people who, having decided to learn to sail, simply walk down to the dock and rent a boat.

- *Reflective observation.* Others learn best by watching a demonstration. To learn to play basketball, such a person might stand on the sidelines and watch others play before trying to shoot a jump shot.

- *Abstract conceptualization.* Some people devise theories to explain concepts and experiences that are new to them. They look at a variety of phenomena, asses their similarities or differences, and then formulate a framework to understand what they observe. People who learn this way rely on ideas and logic rather than feelings and experience.

- *Active experimentation.* Others experiment to see what works and how. They don't necessarily start by jumping into the deep end of the pool, as a concrete-experience learner might, but they might test their tolerance and skills at different depths. They are usually preoccupied with what is most practical and will work best as they piece together various ways to understand something.[4]

How is all this relevant to a leader who is forming an advice network? In two ways. The leader's learning style determines how he describes to potential advisers what he needs. It also influences—or should influence—how he selects advisers. A leader needs advisers whose learning style resembles his own. Less self-evidently, he should also have advisers with different styles. The former will be able to communicate more fluidly with the leader, who is likely as a result to feel better understood. This matters most when the task is immediate, the options are apparent, and short-term improvement is needed with little time to spare. But advisers with different styles will offer the leader a new perspective, crucial when the leader is aiming at an ideal that requires new behavior and abilities. For example, a new leader in an unfamiliar industry will benefit from advisers who think and learn like the key people the new leader has inherited.

Take the case of a CEO hired by the board of a leading life-sciences company to lead it to greater competitiveness. It had performed well since its founding several years before, but growth and complexity on the part of both the company and its industry demanded change. The problem was that the senior people whom the new CEO had inherited had all been with the company since the start, and none had ever worked at an organization of the size they were expected to manage. "These are start-up people," the new CEO observed, "not seasoned managers. But we're not going to hit our targets without seasoned decision making." Because of their functional capabilities, company knowledge, and the loyalty of their people, it wasn't an option to replace them. This leader found an adviser with experience in large, well-managed organizations who had also worked in start-up companies.

In sum, the first task is an analysis by the leader of the situation he faces, including both the "is" and the "should be," and of the forces acting on the current situation in facilitating and hindering ways. After a review by an objective set of eyes, the second task is to determine the type of advice he needs. The third task is to identify the leader's learning style and the ideal combination of learning styles for the network. The next challenge is to construct the network.

Constructing an Advice Network

In putting together an advice network, the wise leader makes a series of sequential decisions. Each decision is a test, or gate, through which a possible adviser must pass to remain in consideration. There are two sets of gates, one to select the right advisers, the second to form a strong working relationship. Each calls for the leader to ask herself a set of related questions.

Selection. The first test is *content.* Given the problems that I have identified by diagnosing my situation, and the types of advice those problems require, does this person possess the right knowledge? The test is whether the adviser knows enough in the right areas to be of help.

The second test is *competence.* Does this person also have the depth of understanding that flows from direct experience? Hands-on experience fleshes out abstract knowledge and careful thought. The ideal external adviser will have helped many others, and will have published his views about what works and what doesn't in articles or books (not just sales brochures), guaranteeing that they have been thought through carefully and exposed to review. Whether external or internal, adviser, he will have had experience in a variety of situations not unlike the leader's. And if he is also an experienced adviser, he will have faced similar challenges himself.

The third test is *chemistry*. Here the leader asks herself what it would be like to work with this adviser. Do he and I seem to be on the same wavelength? The essential ingredients in chemistry are adaptability, listening, feedback, and empathy. (See "Do I Want to Work with This Person?" in chapter 6.) An adviser who passes this test will be someone with whom the leader feels comfortable, and someone who grasps quickly what the leader needs and her preferred style for tackling what confronts her. Conversations will be easy, and the leader will enjoy the collaboration. This sense of chemistry is a reliable precursor of a strong relationship.

Relationships. We have already seen why a strong relationship is important from the adviser's point of view. What about from the leader's angle? Tough challenges—those that have neither mundane root causes nor generic answers—require unique solutions and careful testing of assumptions, as well as the rigorous analysis necessary to arrive at that point. Such analysis is inherently interpersonal, requiring face-to-face interaction between leader and adviser over time. The interpersonal component is less important in routine situations that do not require intense emotional investment. But for a leader who has just been hired or promoted, and who is under pressure to produce results, or a leader trying to engineer fundamental change in the culture of a successful organization, the issues are never routine. And because of the personal stakes, emotional involvement is high.

For these sorts of problems, there is no such thing as helpful advice that is quick, generic, remote, or virtual. No computer program can substitute for face-to-face interaction. Nor can a monthlong executive program at a business school or a weeklong company-sponsored training program. Can these sorts of experiences be useful? Of course they can— they can increase self-awareness, offer generic models and approaches, and explain how others have attacked similar tasks. But for a unique situation and a leader responsible for addressing it, the right solutions must be crafted on site.

It is because there are no shortcuts that conversations are so important. The best advisers are quick to understand a leader's style and strengths, and to diagnose the conditions he is dealing with; they are quick to grasp his image of the ideal situation and to help him clarify it. But such help depends on seeing the leader in his work environment, and getting to know its culture and the styles of the people who surround him. Then the adviser can go beyond diagnosis to craft a solution tailored to the situation, drawing on techniques that he has seen succeed elsewhere. At this point too, frequent give-and-take is a must to assess accurately what can work and what probably won't.

The leader's part in such give-and-take is to clarify the end state; the adviser's part is to forge the best possible means to get there. When they put their collaborative solutions into action, they must make sure that other people grasp what they must do to implement the solutions. This sequence of joint problem solving requires communication, negotiation, mutual influence and mutual comprehension, and ability to see the situation through each other's eyes—in other words, a true dialogue. The adviser learns more as the leader reveals more, but dialogue is even more important for the leader. For one thing, a well-managed give-and-take allows him to explore new ways to deal with the changes he faces without risk. He also hears the reactions and ideas of someone who is likely to be both more objective than others around him and more single-mindedly focused on achieving what is best for the leader.

Like the selection of advisers, the relationship-building task consists of several steps and stages. Here too there are tests, but this time the leader and the adviser must pass them together because they are tests of the relationship itself.

The first test is *practicality*. Advice is of marginal utility if it is too elaborate, outstripping the abilities of the leader and his people, or if it is too simplistic because the adviser mistakenly believes the problems can be solved easily. Either kind of miscalculation can happen if the adviser assesses the capabilities of the leader or those around him carelessly, and/or if the leader does not share enough information or devote enough time. When the practicality of advice is in question, the leader should ask himself:

(1) Have I spelled out the standards I expect for execution? Have I given the adviser the information he needs to provide me useful advice? (2) Did I put enough of my own time into reviewing his ideas as they were being formulated?

The second test is the *added value* of dialogue with an adviser. The best indicator is usually how leader–adviser discussions end. Do our conversations generate valuable information or insight that moves me toward where I want to go? The relationship passes this test if at the end of each substantive meeting the leader knows something valuable he didn't know before or is more clearheaded about how to proceed. The leader's part is to manage conversations in such a way that the need for continuous added value is clear. Occasionally asking "Where is the added value?" will prompt the adviser to explain how his recommendations will make a difference. The leader will know that the adviser is acutely aware of this criterion if he describes without being prompted how his recommendations will further the leader's agenda.

The third test is *dependability*. The question the leader asks himself is: Do I believe that this person will do what he says he will do and will be there when I need him? The leader should feel confident that the adviser will treat an agreement as a promise and will not have to be reminded to follow through. The adviser should report progress without being prompted and help the leader keep track of the tasks they have agreed on. The leader should set the tone for dependability with the adviser in the same way that he does so with his employees—by modeling it. Failing to prepare as he says he will, missing meetings, or changing schedules at the last minute will undermine the relationship with an adviser just as it will with people who report to him. By the same token, the leader must give the adviser feedback when he does not deliver on a promise. If the reason is that the leader was unclear about what he wanted, this is the quickest way to find that out. It is also the most direct way for an adviser to learn how important dependability is to the leader.

The final test is an important indicator in a leader–adviser relationship, *commitment*. The defining questions are: (1) Do these advisers seem genuinely interested in the kinds of problems I have? (2) Do they seem to care about my success? The relationship will develop faster if advisers find the leader's situation interesting to the point of fascination. An observant leader will pick up this level of interest from the types of questions they ask and how intently they do so. Advisers who pass this test will work on and communicate about the leader's problems in the intervals between visits, and come to subsequent meetings with new ideas.

One indicator of whether an adviser cares about the leader's success is worrying about progress as much as the leader does. Such an adviser will listen intently to the leader and pick up subtleties and nuances. The leader will find himself becoming more open because of the penetrating questions the adviser asks, and his active and empathic listening, and will feel better as a result. The more open the leader is, the more the adviser will have to work with. And the more the adviser gets to know him as a person and understand his needs and aspirations, the more the adviser will want to help.

The leader should demonstrate his own commitment to the relationship by conveying that the work they have agreed to is important to him. In my experience, the leaders who stand out for their commitment have been smart advice takers who elicited extraordinary effort and value from their advisers. They have often been those with the most high-pressure jobs. One example is former Secretary of the Treasury Paul O'Neill. Though he bore huge responsibilities and was scheduled in tight fifteen-minute blocks of time, O'Neill conveyed the importance to him of his work with his advisers: he was always prepared for meetings, having thought through what he had committed to; he recalled past discussions in detail, and concentrated carefully on advisers' questions and remarks. By contrast, a leader who often arrives at meetings unprepared, and postpones or shows up late, signals to his advisers that their work is of peripheral importance to him.

To recap, the three tests for selection of advisers are content, competence, and chemistry. And the four tests that the leader and his advisers must pass together are practicality, added value, dependability, and commitment. Each represents a way for the leader to assess whether the advice he is receiving is truly helpful and actionable, and each requires certain behavior on the part of the leader. The basic skill that underlies all of these behaviors and traits is clear and insightful communication. And the key to communication, as we will see in chapter 8, is the ability to listen.

CHAPTER **8**

Listening—the Master Skill— and Other Key Success Factors

CARL ROGERS pointed out that the main barrier to communication is our tendency to evaluate and judge what another person says before we completely understand it. Our ability to listen deteriorates, he added, when emotions are involved.[1] It is when expectations are highest and the pressure for success greatest that the leader must listen most carefully, but at such times strong feeling tends to block understanding. How can a leader manage to listen most carefully at just those times when it is most difficult to do so?

Listening—the Master Skill

Take the example of Steve, one of two executive vice presidents at the company where he had spent most of his career. Tough, dependable, loyal, and hardworking, Steve was widely admired for having pulled himself up by his bootstraps. "This guy started in the lowest job in the plant," said his former mentor, the retired CEO. "In his early twenties, when he got out of the Marine Corps, he went to college nights and just outworked everyone."

Ignoring Unwelcome Advice:
"He Thought His Record Should
Stand on Its Own"

Steve managed people in a way that made them extremely loyal. Among the senior managers, Steve was the most likely to remember a secretary's birthday or send a wedding gift to a former employee's daughter. But he was less adept with those above him. His immediate bosses usually admired his style, but others saw its downside. "A lot of guys thought Steve was arrogant and had a chip on his shoulder," the retired CEO explained. "Steve hates it when people act like they're better than other people, especially people lower down in the organization structure. To put it simply, Steve doesn't manage up well. He had some run-ins with the head of HR and the CFO. They were basically good guys, but Steve thought they would trample anyone who got in their way. He saw himself as the protector, and they had a few flare-ups. Steve was on solid ground most of the time—both guys could be arrogant SOBs. But they probably won the last round."

What the ex-CEO meant by his last comment was this. In the course of his planned succession, the board's options had been to give the job to Steve, the only viable candidate inside the company, or to hire from outside. Some board members appreciated Steve's dedication and no-nonsense style, but few of their colleagues tried very hard to get to know him. The board retained a search firm and set up an interview process.

The leading outside candidate had strong credentials. The CEO kept his vow not to interfere, but he had a talk with Steve. "I tried to get across that he was in a real horse race, that the other candidate was real good and interviewed well. He was very polished," the ex-CEO recalled. "I told Steve that he had to let the board know everything he brought to the party. He had to sell them. He didn't like that at all. His attitude was that his record should stand on its own." Steve ignored the CEO's advice. The CFO and the SVP of HR both expressed strong reservations to the board about Steve. The board hired the external candidate, Norm, without asking Steve to go through a full interview process.

Inability to Listen:
"They're Not Even Talking About the Same Thing"

Steve was bitterly disappointed. Norm, however, quickly recognized Steve's importance to the company and his loyal following. He was the first person Norm called after accepting the top job. But Steve remained remote and did little to build a relationship. Their first open disagreement occurred when Norm concluded that the company's size and the number of management layers were too costly and hobbled its ability to decide quickly to introduce new products and enter new markets. Norm encouraged his top team to challenge this opinion, hoping that open discussion would persuade them to endorse it. But the discussions often turned into arguments between Norm and Steve. The new CFO recalled:

> *Usually, Norm lays out the objectives for the company and then ticks off things we have to fix. The conclusion you come to from his logic is that the structure is a big problem. You don't get the sense he's trying to bulldoze his way of seeing things—it's factual. And he seems sincere in wanting to decide this carefully, and, if we do it, to make sure it's done fairly. If jobs are eliminated, we get people outplacement or good early-retirement packages. Then Steve starts to ask questions. And then he drops the questions and starts making statements. Pretty soon it's Norm and Steve talking, and no one else. It gets pretty heated, and the rest of us just sort of push our chairs away from the table. They're both strong personalities, but they just aren't on the same wavelength. The rest of us walk out of the meeting shaking our heads, because they get to the point that they're talking past each other, not even talking about the same thing.*

Learning to Listen

Norm was certain that there was more to Steve's reactions than met the eye. He also recognized Steve's value to the company and his key position in Norm's efforts to reshape it. "It's to no one's advantage for us to disagree," Norm said. "It will just polarize people and pretty soon they'll be choosing sides." Steve was willing to try to get to the bottom of the conflict and they agreed to work with an outside adviser, who proposed four steps.

1. Separate conversations with Steve and Norm on six topics: (1) the pluses and minuses of Norm's reorganization plan, (2) their respective positions on reorganization, (3) their recollections of their past conversations, (4) what each believed the other's position to be, (5) their views on why the other person held the position he did, and (6) what each had done to pursue or deflect a search for common ground.

2. A written analysis by the adviser of what he had heard. Norm and Steve agreed only on the importance of the decision and its benefits and dangers. Particularly telling were their assessments of each other's positions and their dramatically different recollections of what had happened between them.

3. A review by the adviser of written accounts by the CFO and the SVP of marketing, who had both been present at the staff meetings. In separate conversations with the adviser, each corrected Steve's recollection of what Norm had said and Norm's description of Steve's comments. The adviser then brought the two together to hear each other's critiques of Norm's and Steve's interactions. The two agreed that Norm and Steve had not been listening to each other and had misinterpreted each other's motives.

4. An off-site meeting attended by the adviser, Norm, and Steve, to try to reach common ground or to conclude that agreement was impossible. They agreed to meet on a Saturday so that there were no time constraints. The adviser began by reviewing his written analysis. He then asked Norm to state Steve's position. Steve promptly interrupted to accuse Norm of misrepresenting his views. The adviser asked Steve to hold onto his reaction and not to interrupt. Once Norm finished, the adviser asked Steve not to reiterate his objections but to restate what he had just heard Norm say and to describe Norm's emotions while stating his position. After listening to Steve's response, the adviser said that he had perceived Norm's response quite differently than Steve had. He asked Norm to explain the rationales

for his position, and asked Steve not to interrupt and to repeat what he had heard when Norm finished. Steve tried to repeat what he heard, but omitted points and misinterpreted Norm's intent and some of the feelings behind his words. When Norm was asked to restate Steve's positions, he proved only slightly better at it. The meeting lasted several more hours. In the course of this exercise Norm learned for the first time how the board had managed the succession decision, and recognized the degree to which Steve's feelings about it had colored his reaction to Norm.

Steve and Norm eventually reached agreement about the reorganization, a decision that Steve implemented. And, to the relief of the senior team, both continued to work at listening with understanding. Norm also posted rules for senior staff meetings in the boardroom where the top team met. The first rule was to summarize what the previous speaker had said, and the reasoning behind it, before proceeding. What did Steve and Norm learn? They became aware of how preconceptions and high emotion can prevent listening with understanding, and learned a way to improve their ability to listen.

Like Steve, many leaders judge the advice they receive too quickly, closing themselves off from understanding. As proficient decision makers, they have been rewarded throughout their careers for making quick decisions with limited data and rapid assessments of people. But these very abilities can keep a leader from becoming a great advice taker. When seeking advice on emotion-laden problems that lack obvious answers, quick judgments must be superseded by perceptive listening abilities and self-awareness. Otherwise, opportunities will be lost to piece together the most creative solutions and to make the best use of help. Because it is difficult to do so, especially when pressure promotes hasty decisions, the right advice can make all the difference.

Managing Advice Under Pressure

The giving of advice and counsel to U.S. presidents has been particularly well documented, and can yield useful insights for corporate leaders.

Clark Clifford, a counselor to four U.S. presidents, summarized the relationship between leader and counselor in this way:

> *I have been asked many times, what is the role of an outside advisor? How should Presidents use them? My answer is simple: even if he ignores the advice, every President should ensure that he gets a third opinion from selected and seasoned private citizens he trusts, (the second opinion should come from congressional leaders). Though Cabinet members and senior White House aides often resent outside advisors, a President takes too many risks when he relies solely on his staff and the Federal bureaucracy for advice. Each has its own personal or institutional priorities to protect. An outside advisor can serve the role of a Doubting Thomas when the bureaucracies line up behind a single position, or help the President reach a judgment where there is a dispute within the government. They can give the President a different perspective on his own situation; they can be frank with him when those in the White House are not.*

Clifford points out that the manner in which a counselor's help is utilized depends on the leader's style and personality:

> *For years I resisted any and all suggestions that I join the Johnson administration, just as I had with President Kennedy. However, the relationship I had with each man was quite different. When Kennedy called on me, it was usually to play a clearly-defined role on a specific problem— from the aftermath of the Bay of Pigs to the Steel crisis. Johnson, on the other hand, wanted my advice or observations on almost anything that might confront him. Johnson also asked me to participate in important national security meetings which otherwise involved only government officials, something Kennedy never did. In these meetings, I would say little unless asked to comment by the President—and even then, I shared my views with him later, only in private.*[2]

In 1960, Clifford wrote a memo to John Kennedy after his election but before he took office. Titled "Memorandum on Transition," it offers perspective on past presidential transitions and President Eisenhower's offer to help make the transition smooth. Clifford anticipated resistance in some government departments to the new administration's policies and addressed what he called "the first problem of [getting] off the mark quickly." He then offered detailed advice on control of the executive branch (addressing each of the major offices within the White House) and relations with Congress (reviewing relevant congressional rules and offering advice on how Kennedy might "stake out his legislative program with the leaders of Congress.")[3]

Another classic example of written advice to a U.S. president is William Seward's "Some Thoughts for the President's Consideration," addressed to Abraham Lincoln just as Seward was about to become Lincoln's secretary of state. More confrontational than Clifford's memo (Seward had almost defeated Lincoln for the nomination and might still have been competing with him), Seward's is an example of a subordinate offering feedback and advice to his new boss. It critiqued domestic and foreign policy (after a month in office, Seward said, Lincoln had no clear domestic or foreign policy), criticized the president for spending too much time on patronage appointments, offered Seward's opinion on the seminal issue of the day (the real issue before the country was preserving the Union, he declared, not slavery), discussed military strategy (Lincoln should pull troops out of Fort Sumter to avoid a confrontation with the Confederates), and gave advice about the hegemonic moves of Spain and France in the Caribbean (if those countries did not explain satisfactorily, Seward said, the United States should declare war).

Some leaders would have dismissed as impudent a new subordinate who offered such advice, especially one who had been a competitor. But Lincoln's response displayed his maturity and management style. He wrote out a detailed reply to each point, either agreeing or refuting it. Lincoln was also secure enough to learn from his subordinate's advice; he saw the benefit of making the Union and not slavery the central question before the country (though giving up Fort Sumter was not, he believed, the way to show it). His response also seems to express a growing appreciation for his role as president, perhaps sparked by Seward's challenging memo. Lincoln made it clear that when it came to whether the president or secretary of state should prosecute the government's strategies, "I remark that if this must be done, I must do it."[4]

In his response to Seward, Lincoln also displayed his abilities and wisdom as an advice taker. He never sent the memo (the only copy was in his papers), but met face-to-face with Seward to discuss each point.

Given Lincoln's debating skills and his practice of stating both sides of an issue as forcefully as possible, one can envision Lincoln carefully articulating his understanding of what Seward had said, proceeding systematically through his responses to Seward's points, listening intently to his subordinate's comments, and then listing pros and cons. The meeting seems to have been instructive for both of them, and laid the groundwork for a strong working relationship.

As a result of Seward's advice, Lincoln learned both a managerial and an advice-taking lesson that he otherwise might not have, or at least not so soon. The managerial lesson was to scrutinize Seward's decisions closely. (Lincoln was troubled by Seward's quickness to propose military confrontation.) The advice-taking lesson was to devote time to listening to his senior Cabinet member, whose ideas and reactions were different from his own and, Lincoln believed, in some cases better.[5]

Masterful Questioning and Listening: The Cuban Missile Crisis

A celebrated example of managing advice masterfully under pressure—and more specifically of the power of listening—is John F. Kennedy's handling of the Cuban Missile Crisis. Nuclear war between the world's two superpowers was a distinct possibility. The grave possible consequences of missteps made the stakes as high as they could be, and the compacted timeframe increased the tension. But the most striking element of the crisis from a leadership point of view was how Kennedy managed the decision-making process and, in particular, how he used his advisers to reach a resolution. The sequence of the crisis was as follows:

- *Prior to September 6, 1962:* The Soviet Union secretly placed surface-to-surface medium-range ballistic missiles in Cuba.

- *October 16:* Early in the morning, the CIA notified the White House that a U.S. spy plane had photographed the missiles and a base under construction. At 11:45 a.m., the CIA presented evidence of a missile base in Cuba to a group of high-level officials.

- *October 22:* Kennedy announced the discovery of the missiles. He demanded their withdrawal, ordered a U.S. quarantine of Soviet weapons shipments to Cuba, warned the Soviet Union that the United States would respond with full force to a missile launched from Cuba, and put U.S. strategic forces on full alert.

- *October 24–25:* Soviet Prime Minister Nikita Khrushchev put his strategic forces on full alert and threatened to sink U.S. ships attempting to enforce a quarantine. Six Soviet ships bearing weapons to Cuba were stopped at the U.S. quarantine line.

- *October 26:* Khrushchev informed Kennedy that he would withdraw the missiles and pull back his forces if the United States pledged not to invade Cuba.

- *October 27:* Khrushchev demanded withdrawal of U.S. missiles from Turkey on the southern Soviet border. Kennedy replied that he would agree to the non-invasion request only if withdrawal of the missiles began the following day. Otherwise he would order an invasion or air strike.

- *October 28:* Khrushchev announced withdrawal of all missiles.

It was a stunning diplomatic victory for Kennedy, who had been intimidated by Khrushchev at their first summit meeting in Vienna sixteen months earlier. How close did the world come to the brink of nuclear war? Scholars have debated this question for forty years. It appears that both Khrushchev and Kennedy were in firm control of their governments and determined to avoid using nuclear weapons. Both had seen intense combat in World War II, and knew well the unpredictability of battle regardless of the strategists' intent. As a result, both seem to have worked hard to rein in more belligerent subordinates. But neither leader was certain of the other's intentions. McGeorge Bundy, Kennedy's national security adviser through the crisis, called it the most dangerous moment of the nuclear age. Secretary of Defense Robert McNamara said that the world had come within a hair's breadth of nuclear war.[6]

What is of interest to us here is how Kennedy managed the crisis and how he performed as an advice taker.

Kennedy's Advisory Team

The group that Kennedy convened to advise him immediately after hearing the CIA report on October 16 was called the Executive Committee of the National Security Council or simply Ex-Comm. It consisted of people Kennedy considered indispensable in this situation, regardless of protocol or seniority. Four were Cabinet officers; the others came from the intelligence community, policy-level positions in the Departments of State and Defense, the Joint Chiefs of Staff, and the White House staff. Ex-Comm's fourteen core members were occasionally joined by others who could be useful because of their positions, because they possessed certain information, or because Kennedy admired their objectivity: the vice president, the ambassador to the United Nations, two former Cabinet officers, a former ambassador to the Soviet Union, and the chiefs of each of the Armed Forces.

Given the urgency of the crisis and the grave consequences of failure, Kennedy ordered Ex-Comm to meet secretly. He instructed its most visible members to maintain their normal commitments as best they could, and he did the same. "If our deliberations had been publicized," Attorney General Robert Kennedy wrote later, "the course that we ultimately would have taken would have been quite different . . . and far riskier."[7]

Secrecy also maintained the element of surprise—the Soviets didn't know the Americans had discovered the missiles until Kennedy's announcement. Secrecy also maximized flexibility. The unknown factor was why Khrushchev had placed missiles in Cuba.[8] Kennedy believed that Khrushchev was a rational and deliberate leader, and that, like Kennedy, he viewed geopolitics as a high-stakes chess match in which diverting attention from one's true aims was always a feature of strategy. Kennedy believed that Khrushchev would not take such a provocative step without a strategic purpose, but it was unclear what that purpose was. What was clear to Kennedy was that if Ex-Comm became subject to powerful interest groups, Kennedy would have less flexibility in determining what Khrushchev was after.[9]

How Kennedy managed Ex-Comm reveals a lot about his decision-making style and use of advisers. The rationale behind its composition was to prevent a single viewpoint from dominating the search for a course of action. In particular, he wanted to rein in the military. His experience in World War II had made him mistrust senior military officers and their staffs who were remote from the front lines.[10] The Joint Chiefs wanted to attack Cuba immediately, a course that Kennedy believed reckless. "If we do what they want," he commented to an aide, "none of us will be alive later to tell them they were wrong."[11]

Though he distrusted the judgment of his military leaders, Kennedy evidently never considered excluding them. Instead he made sure that they were counterbalanced by people with equally strong beliefs in negotiation and avoidance of conflict. Secretary of State Dean Rusk said at the first meeting, "We have an obligation to do what has to be done . . . in a way that gives [the Soviets and the United States] the chance to pull away before it gets too hard to do so."[12] Secretary of Defense Robert McNamara also favored negotiation, though he saw to it that the military leaders were heard.

Group Dynamics

The group met without a formal structure or agenda. For several days the discussion was "a babble of digressions and interruptions."[13] It is unlikely that unstructured discussion would have prevailed if Kennedy had not found value in it. Throughout the crisis he encouraged a free flow of ideas and opinions, and allowed (or implicitly encouraged) members of the group to reassess their positions. McGeorge Bundy changed his mind four times in three days, first favoring an air strike, then a blockade, then inaction until the Soviets threatened Berlin (Kennedy came to suspect that Khrushchev's aim was to use the missiles as a bargaining chip for concessions in Berlin), and finally an air strike again.[14]

With regard to the troubling question of Khrushchev's underlying motivation, a leader with a more formal and structured style might have asked an aide for an analysis, or instructed Ex-Comm as a group to generate and present a consensus analysis. Here too, Kennedy's way of achieving clarity and formulating a path was through give-and-take and open dialogue. Describing the group dynamics of Ex-Comm, Robert Kennedy later wrote: "During all these deliberations, we spoke as equals. . . . The conversations were completely uninhibited and unrestricted. Everyone had an equal opportunity to express themselves and to be heard directly. It was [a very unusual style] within the executive branch of government, where rank is so important. . . . The fact that we were able to talk, debate, argue, disagree, and then debate some more was essential in choosing the ultimate course."[15]

An important element of the group dynamics and of Kennedy's decision-making style was his use of a subgroup of advisers. The president's brother, Attorney General Robert Kennedy, and White House aide and speechwriter Ted Sorenson typically met alone with the president after Ex-Comm meetings to review the discussion; Sorenson then compiled a list of Kennedy's options. He did not advocate a particular course, at least in the meetings themselves. As Ex-Comm's main facilitator, Sorensen prepared summaries of issues and questions to serve as a framework for a decision, and during meetings prodded, questioned, summarized, and kept the discussion moving.

Advice Management

Open discussion is only fruitful if the leader listens attentively, challenges opinions and probes for the assumptions that underlie them, and allows pushback of his ideas without intimidating or discouraging his subordinates. This requires a set of skills that few leaders have, especially under pressure, but Kennedy appears to have had it.

"He was not above disguising his thoughts and fears," one account says of Kennedy's discussion-management style. "Moment to moment he would shift from puzzled inquiry to firm command, all the while addressing or ignoring random interruptions [whether serious or trivial]. He used the group to test his instincts [and] nudged [it] toward consensus."[16]

The president became aware, probably through his brother or Sorenson, that members of the core group tried to exclude those with opposing points of view from attending meetings. He made sure they were included, though more participants made the discussion less orderly. Kennedy wanted thorough debate of the consequences of a particular course of action, and some participants' primary role was to offer unfettered and objective analysis.

Use of Questions and Listening Skill

Kennedy was also skilled at asking questions. He gained two advantages from doing so. First, he avoided limiting his options by rarely revealing what he was thinking or what he wanted. He appeared to believe that doing so would stifle dialogue because subordinates would feel pressured to agree. Second, he forced Ex-Comm members to look beyond what was obvious to them. Kennedy seems to have understood that the right question causes advisers to "go active," to think about both the answer and the leader's reasons for asking the question; a declarative statement merely requires the adviser to listen and be patient.

Kennedy used relentless questioning to make certain that nothing the United States did would be misinterpreted by the Soviets and escalate the crisis. The crisis would not end well, he believed, if Khrushchev felt painted into a corner or humiliated. Kennedy's questioning forced everyone on Ex-Comm to put themselves in the place of their counterparts in Moscow. Can we be sure that Khrushchev understands what we believe to be in our national interest? Have the Soviets had enough time to digest the move we just made? Will they see this move on our part as a provocation? Will they think they have to take action to save face? Are we pushing them beyond where we need them to be?

As the crisis progressed, Kennedy's primary objective seems to have been to convince Khrushchev that the United States had a limited objective and no desire to humiliate the Soviet Union. "Nuclear powers must divert those confrontations which bring an adversary to the choice of either a humiliating defeat or a nuclear war," he said after the crisis.[17] Kennedy could simply have declared that this was his intent and told the Ex-Comm to formulate appropriate options. Instead, the questions he asked tested the soundness of this principle and the degree to which his advisers genuinely concurred.

What can we learn about advice taking from how Kennedy managed the Cuban Missile Crisis? It offers five lessons:

- Kennedy recognized that he could not resolve the crisis alone and that he needed advice.

- He constructed Ex-Comm as a vehicle for organizing his advisers that met the intense needs of the moment and the needs of his decision-making style. He required a give-and-take environment that provided information and analysis, a way to test his assumptions, and a process that would continue when he was not present.

- He put in place two people in whom he had complete trust, his brother and Sorenson, to be his eyes and ears and to further his agenda in his absence.

- He made certain that diverse views were expressed and that the process of reaching a decision did not beg the question and lead to a preconceived outcome.

- He skillfully used the power of questions to clarify his options and to enable his advisers to express their opinions fully and frankly.

Kennedy had ready access to brainpower, and he quickly convened a carefully chosen team of people who possessed the expertise to help him choose the best course of action and/or who would implement it once it was crafted. The crisis consumed Kennedy and the core members of Ex-Comm for the thirteen days of its duration. Kennedy was strategic in the degree to which he revealed his thinking at different stages, speaking freely only to his brother and Sorensen, his closest advisers. Meanwhile he managed Ex-Comm adeptly to elicit thinking that was both rigorous and flexible, but reserved the final decisions to himself. Certain aspects of this process are unique to high-stakes governmental decision making, but its general outlines are applicable to decision making in any organization experiencing a period of crisis. The three key success factors discussed in the next section are all apparent in Kennedy's handling of the Cuban Missile Crisis.

Key Success Factors

In the hands of an adept and willing leader, three specific success factors can be the key to unlock the full potential of advice.

- Find and use the right advisers before you need them.

- Give your advisers access to your schedule and to your thinking.

- Take on the responsibilities that are yours alone. Don't expect your advisers to do what only you can do.

Find the Right Advisers Before You Need Them

Wayne, whom we met in chapter 2, faced a sticky situation with his board that might have turned out differently had he made better use of help. But he didn't reach out to his advisers, including his wife, when he saw the first signs of trouble. One reason he ended up leaving the company was that he misread the board; another was that he underestimated his predecessor. If he had made better use of loyal people who came into regular contact with the board, such as the CFO and the general counsel, Wayne might have gotten a warning signal about the board's concerns in time to prepare a defense. Also, it was his wife who pointed out that Wayne's predecessor, the chairman, might have been plotting with the board. Had he confided in her earlier, he might have been better prepared when he met with the directors.

Contrast that scenario with something that happened a few years ago to Nat Stoddard, who owns Crenshaw Associates, an executive-outplacement and career-planning firm. At a conference Mike Rice, a young fast-track Wall Street executive at a major asset-management company, approached Nat. Nat told Mike that his company helped people who were between jobs or had decided to change jobs. Because Mike was on a steep trajectory at his company, Nat explained, Crenshaw could be of no use to Mike until he decided to move on. Mike replied that he had no plans to move, but that even if that decision was years off, it made sense to him to prepare now. He didn't want to wait until he needed Nat's company's services. He wanted to line up helpful advisers before he needed them.

This rule of thumb also applies to leaders who are hired into top jobs from outside. Three essential challenges face someone in that spot.[18] The first is *learning*. The new leader must grasp as quickly as possible the practices, policies, norms, and culture of the new company. If arriving from another industry, he must also get a handle on its customers, economics, and market dynamics. The second challenge is *visioning*. The new leader must use what he learns to generate and refine an image of the organization he wants to create. The third challenge is *coalition building*: the leader must size up existing coalitions and determine which should be nurtured and which should be changed.

Learning, visioning, and coalition building are under-the-surface essentials for the new leader. They are imperative enough to determine his success or failure, but they are obscured by more obvious strategic and day-to-day tasks. Nor are these challenges typically discussed with the new leader or named as primary expectations by the CEO or the board. Even so, because a good start is important, progress should be made on them during the transition period (the period from acceptance of the offer through the first six months on the job). That is when help from advisers is particularly important. But it is also a juncture when so much information must be mastered and so many personal changes managed that the new leader has little time to track down the right advice. If advisers are not in place before the leader begins his new responsibilities, he may not have time to locate help.

The wisdom of having help waiting in the wings became apparent to those involved in implementing large systems during the formative era of information technology and automation. Three troubling scenarios were commonplace: (1) Despite months of planning, the decisions with the biggest impact on total cost and on-time delivery were made just before or just after the budget was officially approved. (2) Many of these decisions were eventually reversed; factors crucial to success had been ignored or misunderstood because neither the managers responsible for implementation nor ultimate users had participated in decisions. (3) Decisions made carefully and with input from the right people came only after cost overruns and schedule delays.

Those of us who worked on the advice-giving side often concluded that we hadn't been brought in early enough. We had had more experience at what made these projects successful than most of our clients, but we were typically hired after management had already defined requirements and measures of progress and decided on a project-management structure. I came to believe that the reason for their hesitation was lack of trust. They were afraid of being taken advantage of, afraid that we would somehow influence the shaping of requirements to our own advantage. Whether or not trust (or our inability to elicit it) was a root cause, not being involved at an early stage made the project more difficult and expensive than it had to be.

Give Your Advisers Access to Your Schedule and Your Thinking

Access has two aspects. The first is allocating time in the leader's schedule. This is partly a matter of briefing his executive assistant or staff aide. The mission of an executive assistant is to conserve the leader's time. The best are experts at triage, managing the flow of information and people while prioritizing requests for the leader's attention; the goal is to match the leader's expenditure of time and energy to his A-item priorities. Even if the adviser befriends the leader's executive assistant, access will not be assured unless the leader explains to his assistant the importance of the work that he and the adviser have agreed to. Also, the best executive assistants are attuned to the boss's moods and emotions. If they sense that he benefits from time with a certain adviser, access will be streamlined.

The second aspect of access has to do with the leader's mind. He must share what he wants to achieve and to avoid, and be open about his true motives and desired outcomes. The shorthand for how much the leader reveals about what he is thinking is *share of mind*. As we have seen previously, the adviser's style and perceptiveness often determine how much the leader reveals, but the leader must do his part as well, especially at the outset. A *Harvard Business Review* article by Antony Jay, published almost thirty years ago, provides pertinent practical advice on how to get the most from an adviser.[19]

Tell Your Adviser the Basic Motivation for the Project Even If It Is Confidential or Slightly Ignoble. Jay pleads for straightforwardness and candor. Though caution is understandable, especially when dealing with sensitive situations, Jay points out that the longer the leader hides his underlying worries or motives, the greater the danger that advice will miss the mark.

Here is an example. I was asked to help a company whose senior managers I knew well, but whose CEO I hadn't yet met. In my first conversation with the CEO, he complained that his people "just aren't up to my expectations." This could have meant any number of things. Because I knew the organization and had an inkling of what was bothering him, my questions followed a particular path. What really troubled him, it turned out, was that his highly political CFO was mistrusted by his peers and constantly battled with the EVP who ran the biggest division; the EVP's reactions were causing tension within the top team and dividing loyalties among middle managers. We could have saved a lot of time if the CEO had just said, "No one trusts David, and the way [the EVP] is reacting isn't helping." The message to advisers is that things are usually more complicated than they appear at first, and effort will be wasted unless they can get the leader to describe the problem candidly. For leaders, the message is that the best test of an adviser is how he responds to what is really on the leader's mind, not whether he can read the leader's mind.

Ask the Adviser a Few Very Broad Questions Early On. A question like "What do you think about my situation?" can have two payoffs. First, a leader who lacks perspective because he is too close to the situation may benefit from hearing an objective perspective. If so, the second benefit will be deeper: a dialogue that stimulates the leader to examine his assumptions so that he gains perspective on the current problem and learns to deal with future problems more effectively. Questions like "Do you think I'm going at this in the right way?" or "From what you've heard so far, is this going to be more difficult than I think it is?" can also lead to insight. So can the "wise dumb question"—the one that is so basic as to seem obvious, but whose answer can cause the leader to consider his agenda from a different angle. Sometimes a question as simple as "Why did you come to that conclusion?" will jump-start a dialogue that produces an idea the leader would not otherwise have thought of.

Another helpful response is "I don't understand the point of what you just said." Its value is to force clarity on both participants in the conversation. A friend who runs a large asset-management firm recently hired an accomplished information-technology manager. The IT manager was accustomed to talking to leaders more familiar with the latest risk-management technology. After each of his meetings with the IT manager, my friend complained that he needed an IT dictionary to understand terms the new manager used casually. Finally, in a one-on-one conversation, the CEO said, "You know, I've understood about half of what you've said today, and I want to understand it all." The IT manager realized he had made the common mistake of assuming that a CEO possesses greater understanding of the technology than most typically do. "All professionals slip from time to time into jargon or, even worse, a specialized use of a general term," Jay's article points out. " You and your consultant have to learn to communicate . . . very accurately, which means spending time in your early meetings constructing a vocabulary. So, never hesitate to ask for clarification by example, definition, or synonym."[20]

Take on the Responsibilities That Are Yours Alone, and
Don't Expect Your Advisers to Do What Only You Can Do

The leader's first job is to be as clear as possible about what he seeks to create. This task has two parts. The first is the mission and objectives that specify what the organization will achieve and provide to its various stakeholders that the current organization does not. This is something that most leaders do well. They are achievement-oriented goal setters, accustomed to defining targets, and they have learned in management-training programs to frame those targets so they are specific, realistic, measurable, and deadline-driven.

It is the second part of the task that many leaders, even the most accomplished among them, often leave to their advisers: the vision part. As we saw in chapter 5, the vision is an image in the leader's mind's eye of the organization that will achieve the mission and objectives. What kinds of people will it consist of? How will they behave? What kind of culture and spirit will characterize it and what will be its values? Will it be centrally controlled or will most authority and costs be assigned to its operating units? How will its major tasks and challenges be handled differently? What will be the organization structure? Too often, by stopping at the mission/objectives portion of the task—the easier of the two—the leader abdicates responsibility for this part of the job.

High on the list of reasons that companywide improvement efforts fail is that the leader has not envisioned the kinds of people the company needs to improve results. He sets ambitious objectives but retains the people who created the problems he wants to solve. Or he recognizes that loyal managers must change, and tells them so, but never describes what they should do differently.

It's particularly dangerous to expect advisers to take on the visionary task. It is the leader's job to define the end state as much as it is to set the mission and objectives. The adviser's job is to recommend ways to further clarify the leader's vision and the steps necessary to get there. As the leader quoted at the beginning of this chapter pointed out, the distinction between ends and means is at the heart of the relationship with an adviser. Antony Jay's article agrees: "You are the expert on ends, he is the expert on means. This is a barrier you cross at your peril."[21] By crossing that barrier, the leader abdicates responsibility in the relationship and also in his role as leader of the organization. Only he can decide, for instance, what a particular process will look like after an operational improvement program, or how things will function once a political problem is solved. If he cedes responsibility to advisers, he will eventually find himself face-to-face with results he is not fully committed to. And advisers who make the mistake of agreeing to do the leader's job run the risk of responsibility without accountability.

Let's return to where we began. As I said in the preface, becoming a better advice taker matters, especially when the consequences are significant and there is little margin for error. I hope that these pages have offered some value to leaders facing such situations. Its ultimate message is that it is unwise and unnecessary to go it alone, but that it is in your hands to make the most of the help you decide on. If you now understand better how to think about advice, if you are shrewder about your responsibilities as an advice taker, if you are willing to examine your attitudes toward advice, and if you are motivated to work at mastering the skills of great advice taking, this book has added value.

Afterword:

For Further Thought

THE CHAPTERS you have just read have not answered every question about being a great advice taker. Additional work is needed to understand fully how leaders can best make use of advice at the most critical times. Three issues in particular warrant more exploration:

- *The responsibilities of advisers.* I never intended to write about or for advice givers, mainly to avoid turning the spotlight away from leaders. But big questions remain to be answered. How should advisers manage a relationship that they approach from the leader's point of view? What attitudes and behavior on the part of advisers will result in the best advice? When the adviser agrees to provide a service related to but outside of his area of expertise, how can he avoid crossing the line and taking on a task he cannot perform as the client hopes and needs? What will it take to provide more training of advisers? How should standards be set and enforced?

   Much can be done on the advice-giving side of the equation, and I hope it happens. I'll leave it to the few good thinkers who have specialized in this area, to the firms that employ advisers, and above all to advisers themselves, who must treat their responsibility to

179

clients as a sacred trust. They must think more critically about their responsibilities and encourage leaders to become smarter and more discerning clients. I also hope that graduate programs that prepare future leaders will teach advice taking as a managerial skill, a step that would benefit both future leaders and future advice givers.

- *More detailed specification of actions for leaders.* *Taking Advice* is not a how-to prescription listing all the skills needed to be a great advice taker. There are two reasons I did not set out to write such a book. First, the necessary abilities (such as listening actively and empathically) are the same skills that benefit any relationship, and they are skills that have been explored thoroughly elsewhere. Second, I believe that the specific abilities that encourage relationships to grow can only be defined precisely in light of the unique style of each leader and the conditions he or she faces. The cases presented here, along with their analyses, illustrate a frame of reference for any leader facing challenging times. I hope it will encourage candid conversations between leaders and their advisers, and that together they will adapt it to the particular conditions the leader faces.

- *Internal advisers and the board's advisory role.* This book has stressed the value of taking advice from both internal and external sources. Discussions of advice usually limit themselves to outside sources, ignoring subordinates, peers, and friends as valuable sources of help. The effect of this restricted frame of reference is that the leader may apply the discipline required to make the most of advice only with external advisers. I hope that *Taking Advice* will open leaders' minds to the importance of help from inside as well as outside sources. Doris Kearns Goodwin's excellent book *Team of Rivals* describes how Abraham Lincoln convinced his former competitors for the 1860 presidential nomination to join his Cabinet. Lincoln's management of these four strong-willed rivals reveals his masterly ability to get the most from internal advisers. He kept all four on his team throughout the war, managed their personalities and interpersonal conflicts adroitly, and retained their loyalty, all of which enabled him to benefit fully from their perspectives and advice. The best use of internal advisers should be examined more carefully. What signs should the leader look for that people who work for or with him could provide useful help? What are the biggest blocks to using such help? Do the most substantial blocks lie within the leader (embarrassment at having to ask for help, for example, or a need to appear in control at all times in front of his people) or in the subordinate (reluctance to say what the boss doesn't want to hear)?

Another source of advice inside the organization that deserves exploration is the board of directors or board of trustees. The role of the board of directors has been in flux since the corporate scandals at the start of the decade. Regulations passed in their wake have had the effect of putting more distance between the board and the CEO who is not also chairman. If the nominating committee has done its job, the board is made up of seasoned, capable people with experience geared to the current and future needs of the organization. These are capabilities that can be of great help to the leader, but they often go to waste because providing advice and counsel is not considered an important part of the board's mission. If oversight is the board's primary role, what should be its advisory role? How should its performance be measured? How can the leader best manage the board if it shoulders both roles?

If *Taking Advice* draws attention to these questions, encouraging further research on the relationship between leaders and advice givers and on the advice-taking process, it will have done its job.

Notes

1. Among these people were John Adams, Dick Bechard, Dave Berlew, Lee Bradford, Bob Chin, Alan Cohen, Martin Ericson, Malcolm Knowles, Ron Lippitt, George Litwin, David McClelland, Mikki Ritvo, Irv Rubin, Ed Schein, and Charlie Seashore.

2. The people who stand out here were Joe Juran, Edwards Deming, Dorian Shainin, Romey Everdell, Bob Barlow, Bill Leitch, Arnold Putnam, and Henry Parker. The work of Keki Bhote, a client and head of quality and product improvement at Motorola, was also very helpful.

3. In the 1970s, two organizations defined standards and established curricula for consultants: the Association of Consulting Management Engineers (ACME) and the Institute of Management Consultants (IMC). ACME was an association of consulting firms that set standards for the profession. IMC was a membership organization that certified individual consultants by means of a lengthy application, an essay on one's philosophy of consulting, and an interview with a peer-review board; the process resulted in a Certified Management Consultant (CMC) designation. Comparable efforts on the organization-culture/management-development side were less well thought through and less durable. In about 1970, the International Association of Applied Social Scientists was launched as a certifying body for organization and management development. Certified by both, I attempted to convince IAASS and IMC to merge, or at least to collaborate. I quickly learned that the task was far more difficult to accomplish than to suggest due to differences in language and approach and mutual ignorance of each other's way of operating.

4. See Bruce Henderson, *The Logic of Business Strategy* (New York: Harper-Collins, 1985), and *Henderson on Corporate Strategy* (New York: New American Library, 1982).

Chapter 2

1. Dan Ciampa and Michael Watkins, *Right From the Start: Taking Charge in a New Leadership Role* (Boston: Harvard Business School Press, 1999).

2. See Daniel Goleman, Richard Boyatzis, and Annie McKee, *Emotional Intelligence* (New York: Bantam Books, 1997), the first book Goleman wrote on this topic; and Daniel Goleman, *Primal Leadership: Realizing the Power of Emotional Intelligence* (Boston: Harvard Business School Press, 2002), which applies the emotional-intelligence model more directly to leadership.

3. David Maister, *Trusted Advisor* (New York: Free Press, 2000). Maister contends that one type of listening and responding shows understanding ("what it sounds like you're saying is . . ."), another is supportive ("that must have been really uncomfortable for you"), while another is solution-oriented ("what has to be done next is . . ."). This third option is Barry's way of responding.

4. For David McClelland's research on basic drives and the nature of motivation, see *The Achieving Society* (New York: Wiley, 1976); *Motivating Economic Achievement* (New York: Free Press, 1971); and *Human Motivation* (New York: Cambridge University Press, 1988).

Chapter 3

1. See Gerard Egan, *Working the Shadow Side: A Guide to Positive Behind-the-Scenes Management* (San Francisco: Jossey-Bass, 1994).

Chapter 4

1. For more on Gerstner's early days, see Doug Garr, *IBM Redux: Lou Gerstner and the Business Turnaround of the Decade* (New York: HarperCollins, 2000).

2. Dan Ciampa, "Almost Ready: How Leaders Move Up," *Harvard Business Review*, January 2005.

3. Clark Clifford, *Counsel to the President: A Memoir* (New York: Random House, 1991), 81.

Chapter 5

1. Jerome Fuchs, *Making the Most of Management Consulting Services* (New York: AMACOM, 1974).

2. This work was done by the Behavioral Science Center of Sterling Institute.

3. This opinion is based on the fact that people taught by McClelland, researchers with whom he collaborated, and those who applied his research made substantial contributions to organization-development theory and organization change practice. They include Dave Berlew, Warren Bennis, Fritz Steele, George Litwin, Steve Rhinesmith, Jim Thompson, Bill LeClere, LeRoy Malouf, Jeff Timmons, Irv Rubin, Dave Kolb, Bill Schutz, Richard Boyatzis, John Humphrey, and John Kotter.

4. Daniel Goleman, Richard Boyatzis, and Annie McKee, *Emotional Intelligence* (New York: Bantam Books, 1997); and *Primal Leadership: Realizing the Power of Emotional Intelligence* (Boston: Harvard Business School Press, 2002).

5. Gerard Egan, *Adding Value: A Systematic Guide to Business-Driven Management and Leadership* (San Francisco: Jossey-Bass, 1993).

6. Dennis Kavanagh and Anthony Seldon, *The Powers Behind the Prime Minister: The Hidden Influence of Number Ten* (New York: Harper-Collins, 2001).

7. Saul Alinsky, *Rules for Radicals* (New York: Random House, 1971).

8. My introduction to this technique was at the NTL Institute's summer program in Bethel, Maine, in the mid-1960s. Tom Gordon is the person I associate most closely with it. A therapist who had studied under Carl Rogers, Gordon recognized that there was no program to train people to be good parents. He created Parent Effectiveness Training, a centerpiece of which was active listening. For more, see Thomas Gordon, *Parent Effectiveness Training: The Proven Program for Raising Responsible Children* (New York: Three Rivers Press, 2000); and Carl Rogers, *On Becoming a Person* (Boston: Houghton Mifflin, 1961).

Chapter 6

1. Bruce first conceived of BCG when he was still at Arthur D. Little. The first company he approached for support was my firm, Rath & Strong. In a very gentlemanly fashion, they told him that his concept, though intriguing, would never fly.

Chapter 7

1. Michael Maccoby, "Narcissistic Leaders," *Harvard Business Review*, January 2004.

2. See Carl Rogers, "The Characteristics of a Helping Relationship," in *Interpersonal Dynamics*, ed. Warren G. Bennis, Edgar H. Schein, David E. Berlew, and Fred I. Steele (New York: Dorsey Press, 1964).

3. See Kurt Lewin, *Field Theory in Social Science* (New York: Harper & Row, 1951), 188–237.

4. See David Kolb, *Experimental Learning* (Englewood Cliffs, NJ: Prentice Hall, 1984).

Chapter 8

1. Carl R. Rogers and Fritz J. Roethlisberger, "Barriers and Gateways to Communication," *Harvard Business Review,* July–August 1952.

2. Clark Clifford, *Counsel to the President* (New York: Random House, 1991).

3. Clark Clifford, "Memorandum on Transition," http://www.jfklibrary.org.

4. David Herbert Donald, *We Are Lincoln Men: Abraham Lincoln and His Friends* (New York: Simon & Schuster, 2003).

5. For a more detailed description of this letter and how Lincoln handled it, see Doris Kearns Goodwin, *Team of Rivals: The Political Genius of Abraham Lincoln* (New York: Simon & Schuster, 2005), 341–343.

6. Max Frankel, *High Noon in the Cold War: Kennedy, Khrushchev, and the Cuban Missile Crisis* (New York: Presidio Press, 2004).

7. Robert F. Kennedy, *Thirteen Days: A Memoir of the Cuban Missile Crisis* (New York: W. W. Norton, 1971), 89.

8. Frankel, *High Noon in the Cold War*, 8–10, 76, 81–82.

9. See Graham T. Allison, *Essence of Decision: Explaining the Cuban Missile Crisis* (Boston: Little, Brown, 1971).

10. Robert Dallek, *An Unfinished Life: John F. Kennedy, 1917–1963* (Boston: Little, Brown, 2003), 93.

11. Frankel, *High Noon in the Cold War*, 97.

12. Ibid., 79.

13. Ibid., 77.

14. Ibid., 99.

15. Kennedy, *Thirteen Days*, 24.

16. Frankel, *High Noon in the Cold War*, 78.

17. John F. Kennedy, speech at American University, June 1963.

18. Dan Ciampa and Michael Watkins, *Right From the Start* (Boston: Harvard Business School Press, 1999).

19. Antony Jay, "Rate Yourself as a Client," *Harvard Business Review,* July–August 1977. Also see Antony Jay, *Management and Machiavelli: An Inquiry into the Politics of Corporate Life* (Austin, Texas: Holt, Rinehart, & Winston, 1968), re-published as *A Prescription for Success in Your Business* (Englewood Cliffs, N.J.: Prentice Hall, 1996), worthwhile for anyone looking to better manage the political side of the leadership equation.

20. Jay, "Rate Yourself as a Client."

21. Ibid.

Further Reading

These titles are recommended for further exploration of three subjects: advice, leadership, and organizational change. There are few books on advice; I hope that *Taking Advice* will stimulate more work in this field. By and large, the most thoughtful published treatments deal with the giving and taking of advice in government and the military, both in the modern era and earlier. Of the many books on leadership, those listed here add value to the challenge of taking advice. Much has also been written on organizational change. Here again, the titles listed have particular relevance to the mission of *Taking Advice*.

Advice

Chase, James. *Acheson: The Secretary of State Who Created the American World.* New York: Simon & Schuster, 1998.

Clausewitz, Carl von. *On War.* New York: Penguin Classics, 1982.

Callières, François de. *On the Manner of Negotiating with Princes: From Sovereigns to CEOs, Envoys to Executives—Classic Principles of Diplomacy and the Art of Negotiation.* Boston: Houghton Mifflin, 2000.

Dixon, Norman F. *On the Psychology of Military Incompetence.* London: Jonathan Cape, 1984.

George, Alexander L. *Presidential Decision Making in Foreign Policy: The Effective Use of Information and Advice.* Boulder, CO: Westview, 1980.

Guggenbühl-Craig, Adolf. *Power in the Helping Professions.* New York: Spring, 1971.

Hersh, Seymour M. *The Price of Power: Kissinger in the Nixon White House.* New York: Simon & Schuster, 1983.

Kissinger, Henry A. *The White House Years.* Boston: Little, Brown, 1979.

Maister, David H. *True Professionalism: The Courage to Care About Your People, Your Clients, and Your Career.* New York: Free Press, 1997.

McAlpine, Alistair. *The Ruthless Leader: Three Classics of Strategy and Power.* Hoboken, NJ: Wiley, 2000.

Nierenberg, Gerard. *How to Give and Receive Advice.* New York: Simon & Schuster, 1975.

Patterson, Bradley H., Jr. *The White House Staff: Inside the West Wing and Beyond.* Washington: Brookings Institution Press, 2000.

Reese, Thomas J. *Inside the Vatican: The Politics and Organization of the Catholic Church.* Cambridge, MA: Harvard University Press, 1998.

Roter, Debra L., and Judith A. Hall. *Doctors Talking with Patients/Patients Talking with Doctors: Improving Communication in Medical Visits.* Westport, CT: Greenwood, 1993.

Salacuse, Jeswald W. *The Art of Advice: How to Give It and How to Take It.* New York: Crown, 1994.

Schein, Edgar H. *Process Consultation: Its Role in Organization Development,* 2nd ed. Englewood Cliffs, NJ: Prentice Hall, 1988.

Sherwood, Robert E. *Roosevelt and Hopkins.* New York: Enigma, 2001.

Walton, Richard E. *Interpersonal Peacemaking: Confrontations and Third-Party Consultation.* Reading, MA: Addison-Wesley, 1969.

Leadership and Leaders

Alexander, Bevin. *How Great Generals Win.* New York: W.W. Norton, 2002.

Argyris, Chris. *Executive Leadership: An Appraisal of a Manager in Action.* New York: Harper, 1953.

Dallek, Robert. *An Unfinished Life: John F. Kennedy, 1917–1963.* Boston: Little, Brown, 2003.

Gardner, Howard. *Leading Minds: An Anatomy of Leadership.* New York: HarperCollins, 1996.

Gardner, John William. *The Heart of the Matter: Leader–Constituent Interaction.* Leadership Papers 1–4. Washington, DC: Independent Sector, 1986.

Heifetz, Ronald A., and Marty Linsky. *Leadership on the Line: Staying Alive Through the Dangers of Leading.* Boston: Harvard Business School Press, 2002.

Kaplan, Robert E., Wilfred H. Drath, and Joan R. Kofodimos. *Beyond Ambition: How Driven Managers Can Lead Better and Live Better.* San Francisco: Jossey-Bass, 1991.

Kets de Vries, Manfred F. R. *Prisoners of Leadership.* Hoboken, NJ: Wiley, 1989.

Maccoby, Michael. *The Leader: A New Face for American Management.* New York: Ballantine, 1981.

May, Ernest R., and Philip D. Zelikow, eds. *The Kennedy Tapes: Inside the White House During the Cuban Missile Crisis*. Cambridge, MA: Harvard University Press, 1997.

Meacham, Jon. *Franklin & Winston: An Intimate Portrait of an Epic Friendship*. New York: Random House, 2003.

Wills, Garry. *Certain Trumpets: The Call of Leaders*. New York: Simon & Schuster, 1994.

Zaleznik, Abraham. *Learning Leadership: Cases and Commentaries on Abuses of Power in Organizations*. Chicago: Bonus, 1993.

Change

Bennis, Warren G. *Changing Organizations*. New York: McGraw-Hill, 1966.

Bennis, Warren G., Kenneth D. Benne, and Robert Chin. *The Planning of Change*, 4th ed., Austin, TX: Holt, Rinehart & Winston, 1985.

Ciampa, Dan. *Total Quality: A User's Guide for Implementation*. Reading, MA: Addison-Wesley, 1991.

Davis, Stanley M. *Matrix*. Reading, MA: Addison-Wesley, 1977.

Deal, Terrence E., and Allan A. Kennedy. *Corporate Cultures: The Rites and Rituals of Corporate Life*. Reading, MA: Addison-Wesley, 1982.

Drucker, Peter F. *Managing in a Time of Great Change*. New York: Dutton, 1995.

Gardner, Howard. *Changing Minds: The Art and Science of Changing Our Own and Other People's Minds*. Boston: Harvard Business School Press, 2004.

Lawrence, Paul R., and Jay W. Lorsch. *Developing Organizations: Diagnosis and Action*. Reading, MA: Addison-Wesley, 1969.

Marrow, Alfred J. *Making Waves in Foggy Bottom: How a New and More Scientific Approach Changed the Management System at the State Department*. Washington, DC: NTL Institute, 1974.

Nadler, Leonard. *Developing Human Resources*. Houston: Gulf, 1970.

Schein, Edgar H. *Organizational Culture and Leadership*. San Francisco: Jossey-Bass, 1991.

Schein, Edgar H. *The Corporate Survival Guide*. San Francisco: Jossey-Bass, 1997.

Index

About the Author

Dan Ciampa advises CEOs and boards of directors when leaders are hired or promoted into new positions or when successful organizations decide they must change to sustain success.

His unique career has combined in-depth experience in leadership, operations improvement, and culture change. While an undergraduate, he was trained in organization and management development, which he applied in poverty and economic development programs and as a social worker. He participated in field research and directed programs on leadership during times of change and helped develop techniques that have become staples of modern management.

In the 1970s, he was trained in operations management, manufacturing engineering, information technology, and quality and reliability engineering. He led the first successful merger of operations management and culture change, a combination necessary for continuous process improvement. In the 1980s, he created one of the earliest total quality approaches in America and oversaw the development of one of the first just-in-time manufacturing practices (precursors to today's versions of Six Sigma and lean enterprise programs), and participated in the formative stages of automation and open systems architecture. In the 1990s, he began pioneering work on CEO transitions and their impact on innovation, operations effectiveness, and strategy. He was chairman and CEO of Rath & Strong, Inc., from 1984–1996.

Ciampa is the author of articles and three previous books (including *Right from the Start* with Michael Watkins) on leadership during times of change, implementing new strategies, operations improvement, cultural change, and CEO succession.